We're Just Not There Yet

Daryl Motte
w/ Seth Conger

Literary Cowboys Books   2012
Charlotte

Published by
LITERARY COWBOYS LLC
1125 Reece Rd
Charlotte, NC 28209

Literary Cowboys trade paperback edition February 2012

We're Just Not There Yet® is a trademark of Literary Cowboys LLC.

For information about special discounts for bulk purchases, Please contact Seth Conger at werejustnotthereyet@gmail.com

Cover design by Damon Sanchez - DARKRIDERDESIGN
Cover photography by Aaron Nace - PHLEARN

This is a work of parody. Names, characters, places, and incidents are the products of the author's imagination or are used fictitiously. Any resemblance to actual events, locales, or persons, living or dead, is entirely coincidental. No reference to any real person is intended or should be inferred. (Except to Beth… she's a dirty scallywag.)

Visit We're Just Not There Yet website at www.werejustnotthereyet.com

Printed in the United States of America

First Printing: February 2012

ISBN- 978-0-9850152-0-6

Dedication

To our parents for giving us a great childhood and upbringing, to our families for supporting us in any and all endeavors we've fallen into, and to our exes for providing us with an unparalleled platform to learn from.

4

Acknowledgements

To our editor Brian: We couldn't have done it without you. From a phone call to a meeting out at the farm, teaching you how to Skype to the infamous 13th hour call which led to the halting of the printing process, it has been a great adventure. You helped us so much learn how to write real smart and taught us how to construct sentences much gooder and stuff. We look forward to you finally reading this book... just kidding.

To Steven: A person who gives us faith in the word "friendship," you my friend, are as loyal as they come, and we're truly proud to call you our friend. Even though we had to cut out your suggestion about the aliens, we thank you for your great mind and patience through it all.

To Vincent and Danielle: I will never be able to fully explain to you how much you helped us, because until you write a book of your own, you won't understand it. Thank you all the same for seeing me through that darkest hour. Remember, you can never speak of what you saw, that was our deal, and you have to keep it, because only ride or die astronauts get to ride in the space ship.

To Trigger: Batting cleanup is a skill, thrill and honor. You were the very first person to read the book for a simple reason, because you're one badass motherfucker and king of the road dogs, we love you brother.

6

We're Just Not There Yet

Daryl Motte
w/ Seth Conger

8

CONTENTS

Intro

A Love Story

We're just not there yet... I really love saying it. We're...
just... not... there... yet. Ha, ha, it makes me laugh out loud
every time, lol. Shit, did I actually just type lol? Man... next
thing you know I'll be typing cute smiley faces... which, by
the way, really needs to stop! We'll have to touch on that
one again a little bit later.

So what the phrase "We're Just Not There Yet"
really says is,

"I do like you... however..."

It's an all-encompassing statement that neatly covers everything a man wants to say to you about your relationship, but just can't find the right words.

You could also use it to answer a tough question...

"Honey, will you go to Becky's wedding with me?"

"Baby, can we go get our picture taken and wear those matching shirts?"

"Why aren't you more in love with me?"

"Why don't you want to marry me?"

"Why can't I have a key to your place?"

Um... well, because we're just not there yet.

Recently, I'd found myself using the old faithful "WJNTY" line a lot more than ever before. The thing I would come to realize though was that it wasn't just me; I wasn't off in some remote relationship vortex all by myself. Everyone out there dating right now, or anyone who has ever dated before, had gone through the same sort of things I was going through. See, how this book really came about was that once upon a time, I too was in a relationship. It was a very serious relationship, actually. It was with a wonderful girl, and when this cute love story took place we were living together in the mountains in Tennessee. We were crazy in love. It was a true storybook romance- for the moment any-how. I had moved from the North, where I was born and raised as a Yankee, all the way down to the Dixieland South just to be with her. We were the ever-classic city boy falls for the country girl love story (cue the Taylor Swift song please). Her very first time flying on an airplane was to come and meet my parents.

So, from very different worlds, and against all odds, we made a go of it, and it lasted for five long years. See, who says I can't commit! It seemed to all that I was a great boyfriend (and I was) although it's quite easy to do when you're madly in love. She was my whole world. Every girl from my past instantly disappeared *poof* with our very first kiss. I was in deep.

I played the role of the tall, dark and handsome prince. She was my blonde-haired, blue-eyed princess. If I showed you a photo of us, you'd probably throw up a little bit! We were that fucking cute. Everyone was cheering us on... at first.

The problem was that we broke up... a lot. Maybe a hundred times, if not more. We were like Ross and Rachel, always on "a break." I loved her, and yes, she truly loved me, but we just couldn't seem to get it together. What was our problem? Well, we had a lot of them actually, but that's not what this book is going to be about (although I'm sure it would make an amazing read). It's about what happened on all those little "breaks" that we took. See, every time that we'd be broken up, I kept trying to meet new girls. I was sad, for sure, but I wanted to move on, to start all over again, new and fresh. I just couldn't take any more break ups. I'd had enough.

Sometimes, we'd be broken up for only two days, but sometimes it would last over two months. It seemed that no matter what happened, we kept going back to one another. Have you ever been there before?

I wanted more than anything to meet a nice, simple girl. I think that's almost exactly how I described it to my buddies. Someone to just be happy with. Nothing fancy. So every time that we'd be on a break, I did my very best to find that girl. I figured that this would be almost impossible for me to do though. I mean look, I had baggage, lots of it, not to mention I was still in love with my ex-girlfriend. I mean really? Who was going to want to date me?

As it turned out, lots of girls did. The problem was that every new girl that I met seemed to think that "we" were meant to be together, too. I'd somehow gone from being that guy who was on his fourth failed relationship (and three of those girls I'd actually lived with) to the most eligible guy on the market? Or at least it would seem that way to these women.

The "one," that's what I kept hearing. I was somehow the "one" who was meant to be with these new girls?! Something just wasn't adding up. I wish I could tell you that this had all taken place in one small, charming town, because that would at least be a bit easier to make some sense of. The fact was I was traveling the whole country for work, changing cities every couple weeks. Well over half of our break ups were because of that job alone. I was gone on the road, and had nothing really special to offer anyone, besides a great smile and some dinner conversation. Yet somehow, all these new girls that I was meeting were falling for me, and not just falling, but falling hard, over and over again!

Was I really that great?

I had a different pretty girl waiting for me in several cities. I must have been amazing... right? I mean that had to be it!

Well, I'll be honest and admit that I had a very healthy ego at the time. Having pretty girls all over the country calling you, texting you, and waiting for you to come back through to see them- it had that sort of effect on a guy. I was becoming quite the arrogant asshole, and I would have been more than happy to continue on with my insane delusions of grandeur, that is until I actually started to share some of these "love" stories with my fellow road boys.

The Lost Boys

They called guys like us "road dogs." I don't know why- or where- that term started, but I knew exactly what it meant. We traveled for work, from city to city, and were pretty much all living the same life: the life of the last Peter Pan. Young boys with a lot of money, and with no real place to call a home. A girl's worst nightmare you'd think... or was it?

The Lost Boys, as it had turned out, were also having very similar experiences in the love department. Girls all over the country were in love with them as well! Well of course then these must have been some easy girls, some skanks, trollops, some scallywags... right?

That was the strange thing- they weren't. All of us were completely different from each other, so because of this, the girls that we liked were all very different as well. Some were single and some did have boyfriends, some were pretty and others not really so much; a few were even married, and yes... some of them were what you'd call "classic town whores," but still, what the fuck was going on here?

Look, honestly, we were all complete jackasses. Total assholes would be a much more fitting name. Sure, I guess that several of us were what you'd call good looking, I suppose. But we were also loose cannons with no stability. We came into town larger than life and left just as fast.

Were we "bad boys"? I guess so.

Was that attractive though? Maybe.

But how could that be what women really wanted? Guys to save? Or guys they could try and fix? That couldn't be right, but it had to be, because why else were we all having so much luck? The best I'd figured at the time is that we were all just awesome!

Years later, I've come to realize, that it was all really just about timing. Just like with the gold rush, Beanie Babies or hair metal, if you'd gotten in at the right moment... BAM! You were golden. Something had apparently shifted in the world of dating, and we just happened to be there at that exact moment. You've heard people talk about the "Wrong place at the wrong time?" Well, we were in the perfect place, at the perfect time! Girls, it seemed, had decided collectively to lower their standards on men. We could do no wrong, we couldn't fail. We couldn't fuck this one up!

So on the verge of *The Notebook, Sex and the City* and "Ross Geller and Rachel Green," dramatic true love was all the rage. I of course didn't figure any of this shit out until a much later time. I mean whoever really sees it as it's actually happening, right? Only now, after much time has come and gone, can I look back and see what the hell was truly going on.

The smoke had cleared, hearts were broken, and morals lost, some people were forgiven, and some never spoken to again. People speak of the 60's and 70's like it was this wild crazy time: free love man, drugs, a sexual revolution, and still when they speak of it, it's with an almost nostalgic innocence. I wasn't alive then, I guess I can't really say. I can tell you this much though, we had drugs, drinks, sex, and rock and roll about 10 years earlier than they did. We started younger, and we did it harder, faster, and with way less regard to ourselves and others. I'm talking about "us" as in all of us. You're included. When did you first hook up with someone? How about watch porn? When did you first have sex? How about try drugs?

The Lost Boys told me some amazing stories from this time period. You know the time I'm talking about ... "Our time."

"This is our time, it's our time down here!"

8

Thank you One-Eyed Willie.

The time we're all living in right now. So when this book idea came up, I called on our Lost Boys about random hook ups and threesomes, drug abuse, cheating, sexual diseases, excessive drinking, good relationships, good marriages and bad ones, too. Did I entertain the idea of writing about all those crazy hookups and one night stands? Yes, I thought about it, but decided if that's your thing, you'll have to stick with Tucker Max. I don't see the point of it. Personally, I don't give a shit about writing down my sexual exploits, or anyone else's for that matter. If I tell you about all the guys having tons of wild sex and about the slutty girls who did all the things that you've heard about (but don't believe people actually do), what will that accomplish? This is not that book. This is about the relationships, the break ups and the lies.

The road dogs' exploits were not told with beaming pride, the exact opposite, actually. Once guys understood the mission of this book, they buckled down, confessed their sins, and confronted the sordid past. We weren't high fiving each other, instead we were asking the questions why, how and what do we do now? Now was the perfect time to make something out of the big mess that we'd left behind. Sure, I'll admit it, maybe I was getting a little too...

"Yes we can!"

I just wanted to make some sense of it all. Guys are a huge handful. I have no doubt (Great band btw, *Tragic Kingdom* is an amazing record) that we have been at fault more than our fair share of the time. So taking that into account, we were ready to travel back into the past and take responsibility for at least some of it.

But then the other half is up to you. Deal?

We'll have some great love stories, some absolute train wrecks, and, frankly, some things that shouldn't ever be talked about. In the end, you may learn some things about yourself, about your friends, and maybe even about your own parents. After all the smoke has cleared I can promise you this much: at the very least, you will have been truly entertained. Can I fix all your dating problems? No... look, I'm not the "One" for you either. After all, I don't even know you or your dating situation. What do I really even know about love, or about life for that matter? A few things, I guess. I'm no expert though, that's for sure. And if you want my advice, you shouldn't listen to people who tell you that they are. They claim to be an expert, in what exactly? Your heart, and how or who you should love? That's crazy. No one can tell you how, or whom, you should love, ever. Not your own mother, not Carrie fucking Bradshaw either, and definitely not me, I'm a hot mess... trust me on that.

I can tell you this though, I've met a lot of different people in my last ten years of full time traveling, and I have been to a lot of different places (*Up in the Air* was my *E! True Hollywood Story*) and I've "known" a lot of amazing and completely different women. Does that count for something?

Well, what would? A Ph.D. in sociology? Sorry, this is not that kind of book, either. This is a straightforward field report from someone who has been on the front lines. Have some fun. It's a great topic that we all spend way too much time on already. If you're thinking that this is all a big waste of time, all I can say is that you may see yourself in some of what I have to say. Maybe you'll be reminded of a close friend. Either way, I think that it's safe to say that we've all been there before.

One

The Beginning

So how this all began was that I was in the bookstore the other day and decided to take a look at the dating book section. Not for myself of course, I'm a guy. I was interested because I'd been hearing a lot of chatter regarding how helpful these books were for women. Some of my lady friends had told me about all these exciting new dating books that apparently "everyone" was reading. They were very excited. Guys coming clean was apparently the new rage. You could learn how to think just like a man thinks or find out why men do all the things that men do. Apparently, "men" were very busy these days, and so simply asking was out of the question. These books promised to have all the answers and explain the great mysteries of man. 1,000 reasons he hasn't called you back? I could think of a few... and not just if he didn't have a phone. I won't go as far as to mention names, but after spending some quality time looking through them, my least favorite book out of the bunch rhymed with "She's Smust Snot into Smoo."

That book made me crazy for a lot of reasons. I could have easily written an entire book just about my reaction to it, but I didn't. I was seriously considering it for about four minutes one morning while showering, but then I figured the damage couldn't be undone, so why even bother. After a few days, I was still mad. Maybe I could do some damage control after all? The biggest problem I had with it, and the main one that concerns you, was its complete lack of...

Truth, depth, balls, logic, lessons, hope, values and substance. Feel free to take your pick.

The point is that it didn't get the job done, not even a little bit. Look, to me it seemed simple. If women were buying books looking for answers, shouldn't they be getting answers? I'd thought so, but after paging through quite a few, I quickly realized that this just wasn't going to happen. Most of them read the exact same way:

"You go girl!"
"Be tough."
"You can have any man you want!"
"You don't need him anyway."
"You're better than that!"
"Take control!"

And so on...

Well, that was sweet, but what those books had forgotten to mention was the main problem of it all… "She" still wants to be with him no matter what she says, and she still loves him no matter what she reads, and she is usually still sleeping with him, and most likely will continue on sleeping with him way after she is finished reading her book.

And why is that?

It's because girls don't like giving up, or being a-lone, even when they know for sure that what they've got is completely wrong for them.

All that aside though, where were all the fucking answers? The titles all screamed, "It's your fault!" "You are being hard headed." "Can't you see it right in front of you?" "Why don't you accept the truth, he's just not that… blah blah blah." Then the books went on to give a million (bullshit) examples of how it's not you, it's him.
Nice try, but the problem was still not solved yet. I was on the case though, so don't you worry. On my next visit to the bookstore, I started looking through the relationship books even closer. A nerve was struck. I was troubled by what I'd found. Book after book full of bullshit! First of all, someone tell me, where were all the young writers? Not young like 16, but under 40 at least? The world of dating changes almost as fast as iPods, and yet most of these dating books were written by older people who were all done with their dating and now claimed to be "happily" married. Barf, eye roll… good luck with that one, what's the divorce rate now? Sixty percent? Well, of those who're getting divorced, more than 50 percent of THEM were doing it before the age of 25! This was a young person's problem, and a young person's plague. It also seemed that all the books geared toward women (which was just about every fucking book on

the shelf) were very, um… how could I put it… gentle. Like if your mother were to give you dating advice.

> "Honey you're so beautiful, who wouldn't like you?"

> "If he can't see how great you are, then he's obviously a fool."

If that's what women wanted to hear, wouldn't they just go ask their mothers?

It also troubled me that the books were written like perfect fucking English papers. Perfect grammar, perfect structures… some even had recaps with key lessons learned, and chapter reviews. One actually had a list of sources! Was all that really needed? Why not just give girls what they were really looking for: the simple fucking truth.

Why was everyone ignoring the fat pretty pink elephant in the room? Not one single book would just "man up" and give a clear, concise answer. It was all soft and kind words, which tip toed around the unspoken truths. And besides all that, how come the people in the books didn't sound like real people? Book after book had these "advice from guys" sections, and each time the guys spoke like proper gentleman. I pictured a dude from a Taylor Swift music video, with bangs, sitting tall on a white horse.

Here's an example of what I mean, this is actually taken from one of those books (but changed just enough so I didn't have to ask permission). The writer had asked the guy to explain what happened on the date…

> She was a very nice girl, and we had a fun evening, I just didn't feel that spark. I really was trying to get to know her but she seemed to have a wall up, I was disappointed she wouldn't let me in…

What fucking guy do you know who talks like that? Do you even know of one? I don't, and I'm a fucking guy!! Sorry for all the f-bombs, but I'm getting worked up again. Let's be honest with each other though, it was big heaping spoonfuls of Ben and Jerry's new flavor, called "Complete Fucking Bullshit," and it was being force fed to girls, who were really sad from their break ups. Sad or not, wasn't it possible that these girls still needed some help? And some answers? How was a girl supposed to learn anything from this?

Time and time again, in book after book, the job just wasn't getting done. Girls it seemed were still losing their boyfriends, making a mess of their dating lives and feeling lost. Where the hell was Oprah?

The simple fact was that women could handle the truth. How was I so sure of this? I'd heard it time and time again from all the different women in my life...

"If you tell me now, I promise I wont be mad at you, and I won't tell your father!"

"Baby, please, just tell me the truth, did you kiss her? I won't be mad, okay?"

"I just want you to be honest with me, I promise, I can take it."

And finally,

"I would rather you just tell me the truth, even if it hurts me."

I could only think of two times when a guy should lie. One: "How many people have you been with?" Listen, we know you lie about it and so we do, too. We'll call that one even. The other is, "Do I look fat in this?" In all of human history it has never, and will never, benefit any guy to shoot straight on that one. Trust me.

Besides those two things though, I was sure that guys would be honest about the rest of it. The guys I knew were talking about girls all the time. Talking about sex, love, dating, heartbreak, having crushes, and so on. But why then in book after book did it say that men don't talk about their feelings? Or say that most guys don't open up or think about things the way girls do?

"Guys don't want to talk about dating, or relationships."

Shut the front door... we will, and guess what else? We do. It's what we talk about more than anything else. Every guy that I hang out with asks for advice about girls, complains about girls, brags about girls, and stresses out over girls. So exactly which guys were these books talking about?

It was time for my Jerry Maguire moment. I had a lot to say and as it turned out, no one else was willing to say it. I would write a dating book. I mean really, how hard could that be? It was to be a dating book to end all other dating books. A no apologies, truth-filled, blunt, vulgar, fun adventure. And why? It was simple. Because women deserved that.

The fact was, we'd all gotten so out of control with the text messaging and random hook-ups, that by the time you added in the online dating and Facebook stalking, people had forgotten how to make this simple boy/girl thing work. I knew for this to work, I would have to be completely honest, and would have to get other guys to be honest. Not polite-honest either... but completely honest!

-Insert dramatic music here-

So with my soapbox in place, I was ready. I would tell the story of dating, from a guy's point of view, with no apologies, no bullshit, no fluff and no excuses. So women could finally stop asking… "WHY?"

So here it is, it's done. You will love me and hate me, all at the same time. In the end though, it will be a beautiful fucking moment in both of our lives.

You will get all your answers, and I will never get laid again, so don't say I never did anything for you.

Enjoy… but before you do, there are some house rules involved.

The WJNTY Disclaimer...

1. Not all guys and not all girls are the same. I know... thanks. Every piece that I've ever written for We're Just Not There Yet has gotten at least one response (if not thirty) from a girl saying,

"But what about guys? Because they do that too!!!"

I know... ok?

Our readers aren't as unique as tiny little snow-flakes. Most people are just people, just in different towns with different weather. A lot of this stuff will apply to every-one, boys and girls... happy now? But at the same time, it doesn't work for everyone *all the time*. People are different, and I'm not suggesting this book could fit everyone's life. The only book that's ever done that before is a dictionary. So, if this book doesn't happen to apply to you (denial is a dangerous drug by the way), that's just fine.

2. "I have NEVER done that before!" is the most common response from girls after hearing some of these stories, but the truth is... we all act a little cray, cray, and often will do things that aren't really "like us" especially when it comes to matters of the opposite sex. We all do it. Even you... if you can't accept that, this book is not for you, and I hope you saved your receipt. Feel free to exchange it for *Water for Elephants* by Sara Gruen, fucking awesome book!

3. "This guy is a complete... Asshole, arrogant jerk, woman-izer, over-confident prick, misogynist pig..." Blah, blah fucking blah. Point taken, and by the way, in some cases I completely agree with you.

4. "He hates women!!" Whoa, whoa, whoa... take a deep breath and settle down... I love women, I promise! The whole idea was to make it much easier out there to date, for everyone's sake. I'd also love it if there were more women out there with higher standards because that would force guys to become better men. If anything, my love of women was the impetus for writing this book.

5. "I don't know where you're meeting these girls because..." Are you sitting down? Because you're about to get served. I have traveled the country for the past 11 years. Most of the time I'm in a different city every other week. I have met girls everywhere because of this circus lifestyle. Girls in every major city and many small towns.

> Rich girls, poor girls, slutty girls, good girls, old girls, young girls, sane girls and crazy girls.

> If you don't fit in one of those groups (lying hurts you more than it does me) then I don't know what to tell you.

6. I was completely honest with the writing of this book; all I ask in return is that you be honest with yourself while reading it.

And finally,

7. You will break up with every single person you date who you don't marry. To get married only one time in your life, which is something that we'd all like to do, means that you will have to break up with 99.999999% of the people that you date. That's the only statistic that I put into this book, but it's a huge one. You've got to understand that fact if you're going to be successful in dating. There should be way more books out there about breaking up, and far fewer about simply fixing your broken relationships. Unfortunately, the opposite is true.

8. By the way, you look pretty today.

TWO

First Dates Do's and Don'ts

Dating. Everyone hates dating. If you say that you don't hate it, well, you're lying. People would rather stay with someone that they're not even in love with, than have to go on dates with somebody new. Being single these days is better than having to go on dates.

That's because dating sucks! It's like going to a super sketchy drug deal. You don't always know everyone that's involved, you feel guarded and self-conscious, and the whole time you're paranoid and nervous like you shouldn't really be there.

Yep, that's dating. The best-case scenario is that the blow is 85% pure and nobody gets shot... much.

Well no need to worry my dear because I've got some great tips for you to help you get through your first big score. Listen, I got this guy... well actually I've got a bunch of guys. They've all agreed to help you so that dating becomes as easy for you as selling pills on Duke's campus... Fuck, you'll practically be able to set up your own booth when we're through with you! No more nerves now because your daddy plays golf with the dean, and they both pledged together with the city's district attorney back in the day! See, I'll teach you all the tricks. The point is this: whether it's a drug deal or dating, it's always *who* you know, that really matters, and that's great news for you, because now you know me!

Step One- The Invitation...

So, you can't very well go on a date without being asked, now can you? The first thing is this: only accept legitimate date invitations. These don't count:

> Hey, let's hang...
> Hey, let's get together...
> Hey, you wanna do something sometime...
> Let's grab a drink...

That's the pussy way of asking a girl out, and we don't want to date pussies, right?

Good.

A guy worth dating will man up and give you a proper invitation. He will ask you out on an actual date. It's called a date because it's the physical day that you set aside to see each other. If you manage to find a guy who actually asks you on a real date- texting doesn't count either- then you aren't off scot-free just yet. If you're not careful you can still fuck this up.

So let's start from the very beginning.

Your phone starts to ring... and it's him! What are you going to say? What do you mean you don't know? See this is already not going well, you're like a little blonde girl who just got off the plane in Aruba. Absolutely fucking clueless! Stay away from the Dutch boy.

OK, the first rule is, without a doubt,
NO GIGGLING!

24

-Phone rings-

Guy: Hello is this Tif?

Girl: Uh huh... speaking...

Guy: Hey this is Nick...

Girl: OOOOOO, hiiiiiiiiiiii. ("Hi" has only one "i," calm down sister.)

Girl: I didn't think you'd call when I gave you my number... Ha ha! Giggle giggle, hee hee...

Boy: Um... of course I'd call you, why wouldn't I? I think you're great...

Girl: Awe thank you... so what's up?

-pause-

Girls, it seems, laugh at just about everything. I almost never have any idea *why* they're laughing. Nervousness seems to be a common answer. Look, *he's* the one who called *you*. So calm down. It's very strange for a boy to ask a girl a question, and the only response he gets is giggling.

Boy: What are you doing?

Girl: I just fed my cat (giggles) Mittens... (More giggles)

-pause-

Look, if you disagree with me about this giggling shit, I want you to stop reading this and go ask a guy friend what he thinks. If he disagrees with me and says that I'm full of it, it's probably because he wants to sleep with you. Either way, you should try to limit the giggles because if you do, it will put you leaps and bounds ahead of the competition. (It's NOT a competition! I can hear you… and of course it is, welcome to life! Next thing you'll tell me is that ALL your friends are super cute! Look, they're not, okay? And nervous laughter is super annoying! You're going to have to lighten up if there's even a chance you're going to learn anything here.)

Just be happy that he called, and that he likes you because any second now, he will mumble out an invitation for a real date. Have your answers ready!

Boy: What are you doing this weekend?

-pause-

What he means to say is, "I want to take you out!" You know this, yet you respond to the question as if you're talking to your boss who just asked if you'd mind working this Saturday…

Girl: Well Friday I'm suppose to go to this thing with my girls, and Saturday I'm taking my sister to see the new Miley movie, (loved the first one! By the time this book actually comes out they'll be up to the third one already, *Hanna and the Sexy Cit*y. That's the one where she sluts it up, and gets prego, I already have the copyright!) And after that I'm suppose to go to this promo thing, and Sunday I have to go to my parents' house, my Dad is gonna help fix my printer. Why what's up?

Boy: Um, I was seeing if maybe you uh…

-pause-

You see! He's already flustered. You freaked him out. If you want a date, then just be honest with him. You're not that busy! Forget all the, "I don't want to look desperate" bullshit. We don't even think like that, especially not at this moment. So go ahead and put it out there for him. "I really don't have anything going on!" Which says, "There is nothing that I'd rather do this weekend, I'd love to go out with you!" Um, I would use your own words though.

Boy: Let's grab dinner, where do you like to eat?

Step Two- The Worst Answer Ever, "I like everything..."

No you don't... so just tell him where you want to go.
Just tell him where you want to go. One more time, just tell him where you want to go. How fucking simple is that?

Never say, "I like everything!"

Guys would rather you just tell them where you want to go. Don't pick the best place, and don't pick a dive. Just a place you will enjoy. That's the whole point. You know where you like to go! Yet girls will let a guy take them out to a place they don't even like. So, if you can somehow master this part, you will be instantly placed into "cool girl" status for life!

Sure, it's great to have a guy who plans it all out, is creative and tries to pick out a great place, a guy who will actually put some thought and effort into it. I promise, I get the whole, "He asked me out, he should pick the place" blah, blah, blah. All that is great and wonderful, when he's actually your boyfriend!

We're just not there yet!

This is a date, no more, no less. Look, he's the guy and you're right, the guy should pick the place. And *he* did ask *you* out, so it really should be up to him. I get that, too. My point is this: YOU can make this whole thing 100 times easier, so just do it already! Some of you will not budge on this point. If you're really going to be that picky this early on, you're single because you are bad at this stuff.

In the famous words of Jerry Maguire:

"Help me help you. Help *me*, help *you!*"

That kid was so fucking cute, right? "The human head weighs 8 pounds..." Well, he ended up hitting the crack pipe... man what a rough town! So just be glad you're having boy troubles and that's all. Because you could be in West Hollywood right now, hitting the crack pipe with that guy who use to be the cute kid from *Jerry Maguire*. Or was it Brian Bonsall? The kid from *Family Ties...* That might be the one who I'm thinking of. I'm not sure it was even crack now that I think of it... But, either way, don't put your children on TV.

So back to the date stuff. He's called you up and has asked you out. And major props to you because you had a real answer ready for his question. Good job. Now you're getting ready (loud girl shriek) because he's picking you up in a few hours to head to Outback (great choice by the way). So we've made it to the fun part, the actual date! Coming up next is how to dress, the car ride and the meal.

Step Three- How to Dress...

Look, he is not taking you to La Boom in Cancun. This is not spring break, and we're not 17. No matter how "Britney" you think your body is, or how perfect your breasts may be, you need to cover that shit up. THIS RELATIONSHIP WILL NOT LAST IF IT'S BASED ON YOU BEING HOT! No matter what age you are, dress like a teacher. A young, fun teacher. A classy outfit will do. Something that says, "I'm hot, but not available by the hour." And please, no nipples. I love it when girls pretend that they have no idea that their nipples are showing through their shirts. Like they just got nipples for the first time a few days ago. I'm on to you ladies. I'm calling bullshit. If your nipples are showing when I pick you up, I'm already thinking about sex and we haven't even made it out of the driveway yet.

All I'm saying is that he wouldn't have asked you out in the first place if he wasn't attracted to you, so there is no need to over-do it. Also, please go easy with the make up! This isn't an occasion for you to try out a little bit of everything from Sephora. Seriously did the M.A.C. counter just puke on your face? In other words, this isn't prom night, it's just dinner. Trust me, you can look pretty without looking like a pageant girl from the South, bless your heart. If he's thinking about you being easy before you've even ordered your food, is that a good thing? Go by the old rule your mother taught you, "You can show off the top or the bottom, but girl... certainly not both." Some girls will purposely not shave their legs, and wear their granny/period panties, just so that they won't be able to hook up on the first night. If this applies to you, look, I didn't want to be the one to tell you this, but I will.

You're a slut!

Get over it. Keep reading…

The fact that you even have to "take precautions" to keep something from happening, is really messed up. Knock it off already. You're better than that! You shouldn't be hooking up on a first date anyway! What are you thinking? I mean really? You're not on the *Jersey Shore*. See, this is called real life, and in real life, the girls who act like this serve only one purpose for guys, and it doesn't include a ring, no matter how much they say they "like it." Sorry Beyoncé.

Ask any guy this simple question:

> "Out of all the girls you've slept with on the first night, how many of them are you still dating today?"

Guess what their answer will be? Yeah, none.

Alright, Story Time…

There have been a few girls who I've slept with on the first night and then ended up dating. Some of them I dated for years even. I have some great memories, and was truly in love with at least two of them. At the time, if you'd asked me, I would have told you that "she" was the last girl I would ever, *ever*, call my girlfriend, yet somehow it didn't work out… shocker, and not the kind that hurts.[*]
    It didn't matter how great she was, or how perfectly we got along with one another. From that very first night an evil seed was planted way in the back of my head, a seed that reminded me (and would never let me forget) how we

---

[*] If you'd like to participate in the WJNTY drinking game, grab a bottle and a shot glass, and take a shot every time you see the word "shocker!"

started our relationship. With every story my buddy told of nailing a girl in a bathroom at some club, or hooking up at a party, I was uncomfortably reminded that my girl and his girl now shared this common hook up behavior.

I'm getting dizzy...

I would think his girl sounded like a slut, but then I would remember, "Damn that's how 'we' started, too." When my buddy told us all about the super hot 20-some-thing-year-old, that he fucked on a pool table after the bar had closed, I remembered how we all laughed and couldn't imagine that he'd ever actually want to date her. I mean that would be crazy. But he did. It lasted a year, until she cheated on him, at a bar, shocker... again.

When she did, all of his friends (me included) gathered around for support...

"I mean she fucked you on the first night!"
"What did you expect bro?"
"Once a slut always a slut."
"Yeah!!" I chimed in with bro support.

Wait... who was I to talk?! I was living in the same skanky glass house. They'd started with fire, just like I had. Well for the next two weeks, I looked at my girl suspiciously. It was awful. Suddenly she didn't seem as sincere as I'd thought... was she up to something? She didn't really go out much anymore, and she was a sweet girl. I mean it had been years since we had our one night stand, but I was positive that she would cheat on me too. After all, they were all the same!!

I know that this is beyond foolish, but that's how guys really think. It's impossible for us to get it out of our heads. It's like having relationship OCD. Well, our relationship fell apart soon after for no good reason, other than our first date sex ghost was still haunting me. Did I ever tell her the real reason? Of course I didn't. What good would that have done? To make her feel like a slut for something that we'd both done, something that happened almost four years earlier?

Lots of guys have this same awful story. What I've now come to realize is that there was really only one chance to make it last with her, and I blew it on that very first night... my chance, I blew my chance that first night, bad choice of words, anyhow, it's worth it to start slow. How it begins will haunt you or possibly save you down the road. You're the only one who can choose this, and I made the wrong choice.

Don't Do it...

If you've done some of these same things in the past, you may be upset after that last section. You may even be in a relationship right now with someone you banged on the first date. So now what do you do? Maybe you're thinking about calling up your ex, to see if that's why things really ended between you two. Listen to me: we can't fix our past. We can't undo it. It's over. Just let it go.

From this point, try to do it right. Dress like a lady and don't put out... quite as much.

> "Yes sir, it's the straight and narrow from here on out."
> - Delmar – *O Brother Where Art Thou.*

Step Four- The Car Ride...

We are driving to the restaurant. The one you picked out. Good job again. This is not time for an interview. Just because we're in a car and we have a 15 minute drive to Outback, does not mean that you have 15 minutes to ask me as many questions as you can think up.

Where are you from? What's your favorite color? Where did you go to school? Do you like babies? Do you like movies? Are you close to your family?

No bueno...

Ask me about last weekend, or about the last concert I attended, anything but stuff that makes me feel like I'm being interviewed for a job. And please don't criticize my driving or music; it's a simple trip to dinner. We're not moving in together.

What was the last trip I took, the last movie I liked, or my favorite bar in town? You don't want to go through so much in the car that you've got nothing left to talk about at dinner. Besides, I don't want to talk about work or my family. And to be honest, I don't really want to hear about yours.

I just met you. Why would I?

Now I have to be ear raped about how your mom doesn't get you and your sister is nothing like you, and you really, really, love your dog... "Like I seriously I don't know what I would do if like something happened to her..."

So you see, all this can be easily avoided just by being chill. It's okay to just enjoy the ride and tell a few stories. Ask a few questions even, but we don't need to learn everything about each other in a single evening. Besides, we're pulling into the restaurant right now and it looks as though there's going to be a 20-minute wait. Aren't you glad that we didn't just spend the whole car ride playing tell me absolutely everything about yourself?

As a Side Note...

People have become so bad at this dating thing that they now have "speed dating" and "it's just lunch" events because people can't even make it through a single evening without completely embarrassing themselves and having an awful time. You are not going to be in that group though, all this is sinking in, I can tell! Sure it's just the tip (great game! We'll get to that one later) of the iceberg, but you know a lot of this stuff already, you just needed me to remind you to calm down and have some fun with it. It's just like the first day of school. Mom says be yourself. Well how well did that work out for you? Never be yourself, not yet anyhow.

We're just not there yet.

Again I can hear the opposition, "Fuck him, how can he say that? Don't be myself? This is the worst advice book ever! If a guy doesn't like me for who I am then..."

Let me cut you off right there. We have a name back home for girls like you. They're called single. You have to realize that being your true self around someone takes time. Rushing it ruins everything, every time.

Would you fart on a first date? How about pee with the door open? Burp after you finish your Coke? Hold on a second... how did your hair get so blonde? And how come you're always orange, I mean tan? I love that contact color btw and your nails are so shiny... Ah, but enough about the real you. Be honest, would you really tell me which one of my friends you hate on our first date? Or tell me what really happened to you last weekend, after you took those five shots of Jack? Of course you won't, and why not? That's the real you, right?

You won't because… WE'RE JUST NOT THERE YET! Well done, I'll get you there, I promise. By the way you look pretty today.

Step Five- The Meal, Yummy...

Alright, some simple things we can start with are...

You're not going out to eat with your gynecologist who you see only once a year (well, maybe three times if you're really wild). This shouldn't be a completely miserable experience. This could potentially be a great guy sitting across from you, who you may even want to date way beyond just this evening. If you're not going to be open to this idea, then why even show up? You've just wasted your own time and his. You need to let yourself have some fun. Nothing is worse than hanging with Debbie Downer on the first date.

Have you ever been out with friends and witnessed a first date at a nearby table as it's taking place? You know the one I'm talking about, the boy who's dressed up a little too much for the Olive Garden, and the girl who's looking away into the light like she's about to be abducted by aliens.* Neither one is talking... it's painful to watch. You need to be ready to have some fun or don't even go. If you're planning to have an awful time, it's going to suck for both of you.

There's an App for That...

Always get an appetizer. It breaks up the meal and provides you both with something to talk about. Remember, have fun! Chips and dip are great, or even something you can pick at like nachos, or edamame... anything to keep you from sitting there and blankly staring into each other's eyes. There are bound to be lots of nerves on a first date and apps can help. Nerves on a first date? There's an app for that!

---

* We call that a Steven Perlewitz date.

The menu is the menu, and unless you're planning on buying the entire restaurant and redoing the whole menu, please shut the fuck up! Of course we could all think of things that would make it even better, but for tonight's sake, let's just keep it simple. Tearing apart every dish and spouting off a custom order to the waiter like some kind of Hollywood tart comes off as very high maintenance. Sometimes the menu will have things that you don't like to eat. So don't order them! I was out to dinner once with a girl who hated cilantro. Fair enough. So when the waitress came for our order, my date was like...

-Waitress walks over to the table-

Waitress: Y'all ready to order? (I live in the South.)

Girl: Yeah, um... so we're still waiting for our waters! And I would like the pesto chicken Thai wrap with the side salad, house dressing on the side, a sweet tea and some clean silverware... and by the way, is there cilantro in any of that? Because I can't eat it, I think it's so disgusting, I mean I hate it...

Waitress: OK, um... I don't think so but...

-Interrupting-

Girl: Well can you check please?

Waitress: Yes I would be happy to. And for you sir?

-I give my order and the waitress leaves-

Girl: She'll probably fuck it up, watch! I won't eat any of it if there's cilantro anywhere on that fucking plate!

When the food finally showed up she combed through it like she was on a *CSI* episode and finally took five bites before saying, "I'm full."

Awesome...

The thing is, yes, you should be able to get what you want. I understand that. There are things that I don't like to eat as well. I'll be honest though, at this point in our date, the waitress seemed more interesting to me. I felt bad for her, nice high school girl... maybe college? She seemed sweet. It's not like she was the one cooking. It's not her fault!

It's always a good rule of thumb to try to and be as chill as you possibly can because your date is learning about you with every single word that you utter. I remember thinking to myself, "If she has no problem being a complete bitch to an 18 year old waitress with a side ponytail and BBQ sauce on her shirt, how will she treat me when I start to annoy her?" At some point we'll drive each other crazy, and because I didn't ever want to be on the receiving end of Miss Cilantro Queen's tantrums, I never took her out again... pity.

I'll admit it, I'm a little more uptight than most... I can hear all of my exes' loud barking right now...

"Ha! Did he just say a little? Okay D... sure, yeah a little, ya think!?"

I like things to be simple, what's wrong with that? I also have zero patience. My mom reminds me of this all the time. She'll say, "You'll never find a wife if you can't learn to be more patient." I tell her patience is for raising babies and puppies, not girlfriends. Believe me though, in regards

to this whole food thing, I'm not alone. Personally I don't e-
ven like it when girls eat off my plate.

It's funny because guys will never admit that they
don't want you scarfing their food. Look, if you wanted a
salad, great. Good for you. But then don't take four bites out
of my steak. I would rather you get your own side of fries,
than have you take some of mine every two minutes. Sounds
silly, right? Maybe it's an old cave man flame still burning
somewhere down inside us. Mine is mine. Apps are fine for
sharing, but not my dinner.

Another common complaint:

> "I hate when she leaves half of her food on
> the plate..."

I spent over a month in Africa. There were starving
kids. It was all very sad. But that has nothing to do with this.
If we're out for dinner and you get a 9-ounce steak and take
four bites before saying, "I'm sooooo full," no matter how
hard I fight against it, I'm going to be annoyed. No guy has
ever said...

> "Man, she ate all her food, what a little
> fatty."

We like a girl who can enjoy a good meal with us.

> "My stomach is smaller than his."

Well, get the 6-ounce.

> "I just don't eat a lot!"

Um...you do now, you ordered it!

It comes down to this… fifty dollars is fifty dollars. It's not about being cheap, either. I promise you that no matter how much money he makes, seeing someone be wasteful is still a turn off, plain and simple. Now if you're at a cheap restaurant, I'm not suggesting that you need to eat all of your French fries and popcorn shrimp. You can just eat your meal. I've been out to dinner before where the bill was well over a thousand dollars, and there were only five of us. Now trust me, at over two hundred dollars per person, it's very hard to ignore the girl, who sadly has half a glass of wine and a hunk of Kobe steak (at eighteen dollars an ounce, mind you) cooling on her plate.

I didn't care at all about the money; it was the simple fact that one hundred and sixty dollars worth of cow should be eaten! Even if it's not your intention, you will come across as being unappreciative.

So order what you're capable of eating. Skip lunch if it helps. I remember my favorite first date of all time was with a tiny girl (she was tiny, not young) who put down over a pound and a half of king crab legs, and ate her whole baked potato! And then after dinner, she still let me take her out for ice cream. Way cool girl, she was my "Allie," we were birds.

Some girls take an easy out. It's not about what they're able to eat, it's about their own complete lack of adventure. Which brings us to the most annoying dinner order of all time: grilled chicken salads.

Ordering that just reminds us of every other girl before you who has ordered the same thing. You're a grown up now, you should be able to order real people food. My high school dates all ordered chicken salads. High school girls order salads because they're super picky eaters. Do you really want to remind me of my high school girlfriend?

"But I like eating salads!"

Well, I'm not interested in dating a rabbit. I would like you to be able to eat people food, not just lettuce! Some of this seems really harsh, and even while I'm typing it out, I feel like a complete dick head, but I still think it's worth talking about. We're planting seeds so that you'll have a happy dating life from here on out. Does it really come down to you not ordering salads every time you go out to eat? No, of course not. However, I think little steps to get you out of your comfort zone (think Angelina instead of a Jennifer) will help.

I know, you love Jennifer! Everyone's "Team Jen." I'll be honest with you though, I just don't get what all the fuss is about. She was cute for like a second, but now she's kinda blah and can't keep a man. She does have a rocking body though, I'll give her that! What she really needs are some hobbies. I mean besides getting dumped and making bad movies, what the hell does she do all day? I'm telling you, that woman has got to be a nightmare to be around! Even Owen wanted to kill himself after spending too much time with her!

It's a joke... settle down. I'm sorry, is he a friend of yours?

The point is that even after you marry, you will, in a way, still be dating your husband. So all of this carries over. You want to keep growing as an individual, and your guy should be growing, too. If he is still playing Madden daily and hitting up dollar beer night, you took a wrong fucking turn somewhere way back on "choosing a dude" street. Let's have a little chat with Garmin and see where we went wrong here...

Can I just say that Garmin drives me fucking crazy! It never gets it all the way right. Kinda like driving your hammered friend home who's trying to give directions to another friend's house that he's only stayed at once in his life. Once Garmin tried to get me to drive into a river! I swear Garmin was trying to kill me that night! I just wish it would be honest and say stuff like:

> "Go this way if you want to."

> "I think this could be right? It seems right, I'm not really sure though."

> "Your choice, I think we're lost."

> "Um…"

> "Look, I didn't realize you meant *Chicago*, Chicago. My bad."

Damn you Garmin.

Anyhow, the things that you'll find attractive in a mate at twenty usually disappear once you arrive at thirty. So do your best to pick a guy who's on his way to becoming a real man!

Before we go onto the rest of the evening, I have one more thing about the "where to go" part of the date. The worst first date place to go ever, ever, *ever* is a movie. It's not social in the least, and it's never as great as a fun night out together where memories can be made. Assuming that you end up dating this guy for a while, or even maybe end up getting married to him, who wants to look back and remember that the first time you went out together was to see that awesome new Michael Cera movie. You know the one, where Michael Cera plays a love-struck teenager who overcomes impossible situations to win the indie girl of his dreams (here's a little career advice for Mr. Cera: let's try and start branching out a bit, shall we! They can't all be *Super Bad*). The other bad thing about movie dates is this: a dinner and movie is what every high school boy comes up with as his fail-safe Friday night date plan. You will see e-nough movies throughout the life of this relationship, there's no need to start too early.

Step Six- "Thank You For Dinner"

It's that simple, really. There's no need to offer to pay, and even less need for us to argue about it.

"I insist... No I insist... Please just let me pay the tip... No, no, I got... Ok look, I'm a big girl, I can buy my meal... No, I want to get it... Ok..."

That was even exhausting to type. If you really want to help him out, offer to pay if you happen to go out somewhere after dinner, for, say, ice cream or coffee. Thank you is a very important part of the date. It really sucks when a girl waits until the very end of the night- or, even worse, the next day- to say it. Actually no, the very worst is having her forget all together! So after the bill is paid just say,

"Thank you for dinner, it was very good."

He's happy, you're happy, everyone is happy. Let's move on.

Now it's after dinner, and any guy worth a second date will take you out somewhere. If the dinner went well, great, I'm happy for you. If not, well no worries because we still have the rest of the evening. All kinds of things can go wrong on a date, but almost every horror that you can think up can be smoothed over (unless of course you puke in his car, or in my case, my brand-new, only-had-it-for-two-days car, but that's a story for another time). I would say that the only date night horror you really can't bounce back from is getting wasted-face with him. He may want to have a drink or go to his favorite bar. That's all fine and dandy. So have a drink, or maybe even three. But no matter what, don't over do it...

Don't be that girl!

"What girl is that?"

This one: The drunk storyteller version of you...

> "OMG, so... ok, me and my girls went to this bar last Friday, Rogues Gallery, and they had this guy there, right? He was spinning, his name was Kid Cut Up, and Stephanie knew him I guess... so we requested a song, and he was all like, 'Look, I don't take requests.' But then she whipped out her nipple... and so then, anyway, he like played this Lil Wayne song, that one that we always sing... hot banana... hot banana... and so then my friend Beth, she started singing it right, but then she took a drink and we're all laughing so hard, that it shot out of her nose! (laughing, snorting) OMG, like fricking Jack shooting out of her nose! OMG, but it was so funny because we had glitter on and she was like, 'Fuck, my glitters getting all jacked up!' Get it? Jacked up? And I had my little backpack on and so we danced to like every song..."

If he's still sitting across from you after you just ear raped him with this awesome story, you're either extremely hot or he's banking on a blowjob at the very least. Look, getting completely fucked up is fine for you and your girls. Not for you and your date. And never ever, ever, go back together to his place- or your place for that matter. Trust me, you two won't just "hang out," it's never for "only a minute" and he doesn't really need to "show you" anything (well, *he* thinks he does. Guys add an inch for every shot they consume) either. All that being said though, the absolute worst idea, the one that just cannot happen, is for either of you to spend the night!

Never ever?

Never ever ever??

NEVER EVER!!!!

We will come back to this one. I should have made this book like a *Choose Your Own Adventure* book.

"Staying the night?" Turn to pages 59, 66, 121 or 200.

"Feeling tipsy?" Turn to pages 45, 79, or 108.

"If you want to end this date," turn to pages 74, 130, or 208.

Those books were fucking great man. I also got down with some Judy Blume, *Tales of a Forth Grade Nothing,* and of course, *Super Fudge...* Really? Come on... How about Beverly Cleary's *Dear Mr. Henshaw?* You didn't read *Ribsy* or *Ramona Quimby* either? That's so sad. Well you really should have! Best fucking books ever! Of course I don't have kids yet, but if the condom ever breaks, I'm getting my children those books for sure! Anyhow, we are almost at the end of the date! So let's continue on...

He's a Nice Guy... Maybe

Throughout the evening it may seem that your date is a very polite, sincere, sweet, thoughtful, well-behaved man. This is not necessarily a trap. It's true that some guys are complete fucking actors who will spend all night being the "good guy" before finally trying to get their hand down your pants or up your shirt (Steven, here is your shout out that you asked for!) in the car. I know, we suck. The thing is, there are still some really good guys out there, and just because you've been out with Johnny sneaky hands in the past, doesn't mean that this new guy is related to him. Niceness does not always equal horny-ness! Sometimes he's just a good guy. I've actually had girls say to me after opening a door for them on our date,

> "Whoa, pulling out all the stops tonight... hope you're not thinking that this will help you get lucky."

> "Bet you've never done that before."

> "Are you trying to get me to sleep with you?"

It comes down to this: don't bring your past dating experiences with complete sketch balls to our night out together. Leave them at home in your box marked "Stupid shit I shouldn't talk about." I'm sorry that you've dated boys who didn't know how to treat a girl right. Welcome to grownup land. I open doors, hold doors open and pull out chairs. I do it for my mother and I'm going to do it for you, too. That's how a man is supposed to act. It doesn't mean that I'm trying to fuck you!

By the way, if the chivalry drops off after only a few dates, ditch him because that's a red flag. Also, if you're sitting there the whole time thinking, "Hmmm, I think he'd be a great actor!" you're most likely right. Girls seem to have a fairly good bullshit meter, especially in regards to dirt bags. Why they still choose to date these guys? No fucking clue. I would just like to say it again though, some guys were raised properly, and real gentlemen do still exist, so be open to the possibility.

Step Seven- The End of the Night...

Headed to the drop off spot, and both of you are more nervous than Charlie Sheen after having another 19-year-old girl call him up and say,

"Um, hey Charlie, we need to talk..."

This is really the most important part of the evening, the make or break moment of it all. Everything that's gone well so far can come undone just like a sweater (Weezer reference). I probably should've just "Tarantinoed" the whole date process and started at the end.
Too late for that now, we're already here.

I know that not every date is a boy and girl, riding around in a car. In fact, some dates are two boys, in which case all of the same rules will apply, only throw in a fiercer wardrobe and a cock ring. I didn't mean to leave all the queens out... you're loving this book right? I know us straight boys are silly! Don't even get me started on y'all though... I mean *bears*? Someone please explain that shit to me? Speaking of assholes, let's talk about Ellen. Really? If she were any more confused, she'd be Cher's son! Anyway I do have some advice for the sweet boys out there, and my advice to you is this: if you're ever with a guy who insists that he's a "top" only, trust me, that short dick bitch has a wife and child out there somewhere. Remember that I'm the one who told you that. Oh, and never date someone "white" after Labor Day.

So anyhow, at the end of the date an important choice is often left lingering: how do you get back to where it started? Did you drive separately? Did you meet up and take one car? Maybe you took the subway, or Marta. How about in the interest of keeping it very simple we stick with the car/doorstep goodbye.

"Goodbye on the doorstep?"

"What… are we on the set of a WB show now?"

Look, I know the difference between real life and *Dawson's Creek*. In real life, Joey wouldn't give Tom Cruise the time of day. Savekatieholmes.com. It's not a real website yet, but it should be.

So for this goodbye to be successful, it's got to go quickly. You need to be ready and have a decent plan. My plan, the one you're going to follow from now on, is short and sweet. No matter what happens or what time it gets to be, you cannot have him come inside! Not even for a second.
Guy secret coming up in 3… 2… 1…

I hate to admit this, but guys are always way more nervous than girls when it comes to this goodnight thing. Good guys are anyway. It's because without fail, every single time, we have no clue how to read you at the end of the night. Sure, we have a lot of hopes and wishes, but it's just like Mick said, "You can't always get what you want."
So we'll wait around for you to make it crystal clear to us, just how you'd like us to proceed. This is why "Goodnight," which should take less than five minutes, takes an uncomfortable twenty-nine. Let's work through it, and you may agree that my way is a bit easier for everyone involved.

Okay, so you just pulled up to your place, or his, wherever… first, say, "Thank you, I had a really nice time, you're a great date, I had so much fun with you, let's do this again soon, blah, blah, blah."

Sounds so easy right? Well, It would be except for what happens is, it turns into this whole awkward...

"Should I kiss her?"
"Is he going to kiss me?"

1. Don't kiss in a car. It's tacky.
2. YOU have to take control. If you don't, this could take all night, and we're going to miss *Modern Family*.

After you say, "Thank you!"
Ask him, "Will you please walk me to my door?"

If he does it, then he's a good guy. If he doesn't, then he obviously didn't have as great of a time as you did. In that case, you don't want to be kissing him anyway. So once you're there, at whatever door it is that you need to be at, if you'd like a kiss, then just ask for it!
Sounds crazy right?

I just heard a girl in the back of the room say, "Fuuuuck that!"

Listen, guys have no problem with, and would in fact love it, if a girl said to them, "Give me a kiss." It lets him know that it's okay with you. You also, from time to time, will get the other guy, the one who just wants to put his tongue in your mouth (Hi Rufio) and doesn't really care how you feel about it. I would say though that any stand up guy, any guy worth dating, is beyond stressing out during this brief walk to your door. So give it a try!

Say, "Give me a kiss."

-Kissing sounds, tongue, slurping-

Whoa, eeeeeasy there Sea Biscuit.

Again, keep it sweet. Think church tongue! Most guys have had the tongue bandit queen on the steps before, or the surprise blowjob on the couch girl. We don't say nice things about those girls, either. We're usually on the phone with a buddy, recapping it all, before we've even made it back home. Trust me, you do not want to remind him of either one of those girls. So keep it sweet and leaning toward PG, and he'll be hooked, I promise.

If He Asks to Come Up...

Boy: "Aren't you going to invite me up?"

You: "I'm sorry, I'm not that kind of girl."

-Loud Buzzer Sound-

Way wrong answer!

Don't ever get into playing the whole assumption game with him. It doesn't really matter what he says because he's not coming up regardless (I'll tell you why soon enough, turn to page 212 if you just can't wait any longer).

Just say this instead:

"I'm still getting to know you. So when can we go out again?"

Checkmate! Well played pretty girl.

If he's still being a persistent little prick about it, and keeps trying to kiss you, or even worse says, "Come on baby. Please?"

First of all… you're not his baby! It's time to hit him with the old fool proof:

"I'm sorry, we're just not there yet!"

Double checkmate. You win! Assuming it all went well, and he's decided not to pull the asshole card, your last power move is right now.

Tell him that YOU will call him tomorrow (that is, if you want to. If not, then just say a simple good night and go inside).

If you do the first part though, then you won't have to sit around all day and wonder if, or when, he's finally going to call you. Every dating book seems to paint you as a silly high school girl, waiting by the phone, eating ice cream, or Hot Pockets or whatever. First of all, don't eat Hot Pockets, or any other prepackaged microwave meal… it will just make you fat! Remember, nothing tastes as good as skinny feels! Second of all, who the fuck still has a house phone these days? Chalk up yet another reason as to why all those dating books completely missed their mark! You're not that girl anymore, all right? You're a grown up now, and those books all seem to paint you like a cray cray, pimpled-faced, over-emotional teen and those books are, well, wrong. I'm right, and there is nothing wrong with simply saying…

"Goodnight, I'll call you tomorrow."

I can hear the whiny girls now, even after we just went through that entire section. They're saying, "But I don't want to seem desperate!"

Let's play a game. It's called shut the fuck up. You go first.

I'm sorry, but please, can you just be quiet for a second? You don't look desperate. Trust me! Plus, normal guys don't give a shit about that stuff anyway. If anything, you'll come off as a girl who just wants to see him again, and one who isn't a make out Mary! You are beyond golden at this moment in time, and if you want to keep it that way, until the next date you have with him, there are a few things that no matter what, you absolutely should not do…

> Text him goodnight right after he drops you off.
>
> Ask him exactly when he's going to call you.
>
> Make him "promise" to call you.
>
> Call him more than one time in the first 24 hours after your date.
>
> Text him more than once the very next day.

You get the basic idea. Just don't be you! I'm joking. Well, sort of. Don't be the overbearing, insecure version of you! Easier said than done, I know. We can thank your mother for that one. The goodnight hopefully went off without a hitch because I'm all out of suggestions for you, and with any luck you didn't end up getting pregnant tonight. Date two is set up for next week ☺. I think you're ready!

So that covers the first date, and now we'll move on from here to what's referred to as, well, actual dating. It's going to get a bit tricky. We'll throw in things like friends, bad dating habits, deal breakers and everything else. Basically it's the whole rest of the book. Before we go anywhere though, it's now time for us to come back to the reason why you shouldn't ever have sleepovers with boys!

Remember...

Never ever, ever, go back to his or your place. Trust me, you two won't just "hang out," it's never for "only a minute" and he doesn't really need to "show you" anything either.

Never ever?

Never ever, ever?

NEVER EVER!!!!

-Warning-

This next section is going to get pretty rough, and it will go against everything that you and your friends, and Carrie fucking Bradshaw and her friends, are doing right now. By the way, she should have totally picked Aidan! I mean really, how could she have picked Big, right? Aidan was perfect for her and he really cared about her besides. I love that show. I've seen every single episode from every season and then went to see both of the movies, twice (with different girls)! The fact that she didn't pick Aidan either time was actually the most realistic part of the whole show. She passed up the good guy to choose the jerk instead. The classic dumb girl move. Big was not right for her at all, and he really was a "Big" jerk! Call it love if you want to, but it's love without respect, if there even is such a thing as that. I hated that she picked Big and not Aidan... I still hate it... I miss Aidan.

You don't have to like this next section or agree with all of it, but if you want to learn something and really reflect on your past and current dating life, by all means strap in and come along for the ride. If you've already got it all figured out, that's fine. You may want to come back and see me when you're finally ready to listen. Maybe in about 5 years, when you're a bit older, and after you've become divorced, and are a single mother, you may find that you weren't as open to some of this stuff at the time, and that I was actually right. I'll still be here for you though, don't you worry.

In all seriousness, this is about as dark as the book will get. It will not be pretty roses, or sweet candy corn, and if you're having a great day right now, or are in a super good mood, you should probably just stop reading right now and put it down. Please, can you just trust me?

Why are you reading this line!? Didn't we just have this conversation?

You're going to read it anyway, aren't you?

Fine then, I'm not the boss of you. I'll tell you what... I get it. All right. Fine. I'm an emotional cutter too, so let's at least do this together then. It will be an interactive experience. I'm not sure it's ever been done before, but I think it could work. I need you to go right now and get us a snack and some wine, and then get ready for some cinematic magic.

-This is the time to go and get some snacks-

I want you to watch *The Notebook* or maybe *My Sister's Keeper* or *Deep Impact*. I end up calling my Mom every single time I watch *Deep Impact*- and you should call yours, too! Or maybe you could watch a TV show like *Grey's Anatomy* with Dr. Bailey when the elevator's broken... or when George dies... and... everyone... excuse me for a moment...

Whew... ok...
I'm back, sorry about that.

It's whichever movie or TV show will get you into that sad, emotional, tear-filled place where the only thing you want in the entire world is just to have real love in your life.
You know which one I'm talking about.
So go and get your "cry movie." Put it on, watch it and come right back here as soon as it's over and read the next section, start to finish. It will be just like listening to Pink Floyd during *The Wizard of Oz*, only with a book, and without any Pink Floyd.

58

Just do it because I asked you to. I need you to trust me on this.

Sleepovers...

I know tons of girls and guys, (yes, we're both guilty) who've made it a habit of having just as many sleepovers as they do dates. This trend has got to stop.

> "But we didn't really hook up…"
> "Well, I didn't want him to have to drive…"
> "It was already three in the morning…"
> "Well, we fell asleep watching a movie…"
> "But I love to cuddle…We didn't even have sex…"

There are a million reasonable excuses for having a sleepover, but let me give you the one, and only reason why you shouldn't:

Married people sleep in the same bed together.

I know that this is a hard concept, so I'm going to attempt to lay it out nice and easy for you, just like when your mother picked out something for you to wear to school and then set it neatly on your bed the night before.

It all has to do with the battle between sex and intimacy. Sex is amazing and it's very important to any relationship.

Sex can occur almost anywhere, too. It's possible to have sex in a loving bed and call it making love, but it's also possible to have sex in a pool, car, park, shower, on your boss's desk, in the bathroom at a club, at the zoo near the penguin's tank, even in the glass elevator of a very nice hotel.

Or so I've heard.

It's just sex though. That's the problem. People have sex everyday with people that they don't even really like. Having sex with someone these days really means nothing.

It's sad to see it this way, and somehow it feels really fucked up, I agree, but there's no use in pretending. It's where we are now as a culture. We thought that the '70s were crazy? Well, welcome to modern day dating. It's a complete fucking train wreck, and it's spreading fast, HazMat is on the scene and CNN is already going to air.

Girls and guys spend their teens and twenties crashing through relationships, often ignoring all the scars. Girls sleep with four or five guys, and that's just on spring break. Guys often cheat on every single girlfriend that they have, using the rationalization, "I'm young bro, what did you expect?"

Then just a few short years later, we'll try to make our relationships work, but it's really hard, especially with our heads filled up with years of carnage. Girls will throw themselves into serious relationships after having a slew of one-night stands, two black out nights with a side of, "Yeah I cheated on him. So what? He did it too…"

Then they actually wonder why relationships are so tough.

It's our fault. We try our best to pretend and then lie to ourselves that sex can be a special bond or something meaningful. But it's just not anymore. Of course, I know that this may not really apply to you, but it's just like when you were little and your brother or sister got in trouble for something. Sometimes even when you didn't do it, you still got the lecture from mom anyway.

That's not fair? Well neither is pretty girls marrying for money, now is it? Suck it up, you're perfect, I know. Ok, feel better now?

Let's continue shall we?

We're now in a time where girls and guys have had ten, even twenty different sex partners before they've even gotten out of high school. Sexting is the new flirting, and kids get their first blowjob on a school bus. They've even witnessed porn without... hairy bush! It's a dark time. Young teens are entertained daily by programs filled with hooking up, random sex and competitions for "true love" as their plot.

Our parents had *The Dating Game* we have *The Bachelor*? They had Frankie and Annette we had Nick and Jessica, who are divorced now by the way! They had Marsha Brady and we've got fucking Snooki? They got married in churches, and we get married on television shows or by Elvis in Vegas.

How can anyone not see it? There are people out there who don't have sleepovers. They believe it's wrong and so they abstain. They're very selective with the few partners they have, and some even wait until marriage. Guess what else? They don't need dating books.

I'm not going to get all rah rah God on you, that I promise. Which reminds me...

-God is good, God is great - Amen.

Stay with me because we're going somewhere good with all this. I know it's a bit depressing. You wanted it to be funny and witty the whole way through? Go and read some of Chelsea Handler's shit (I promise it's good, I'm a huge fan). I don't have much to joke about on this particular topic though, so it's time for a little seriousness. No more jokes. Way too often we make light and joke about this dating stuff, but behind that front, people are getting their fucking hearts ripped out! No one seems to ever want to talk about it in a serious way, but it's very important that we do, because we can all afford to make some major improvements.

Remember we started this whole thing off with the reasons why you shouldn't ever spend the night together?

Never ever?

NEVER EVER!!!

Here is another reason why: spending the night in a bed is an act that is extremely intimate between two people. Intimacy is the key to it all. It's the lack of intimacy that ends marriages every single day. Ironically, intimacy is what kept our grandparents together, strong and married, for what seemed like... for-ev-er.

Intimacy is our last saving grace. It's all we really have left. We've got to protect it like we would John Conner, if he were real. Sure, we've ruined sex, but we still have intimacy.

See, the problem is that when you spend the night with a boy, and another, and yet another, you've had an intimacy that even amazing sex can't give you.

> "So what then? Have sex and just have him leave?"
> "I'd feel like a whore!"

No comment.

Then probably just don't have sex. Look, if you have sleepovers with every boyfriend you've ever had, what have you gained? You've been playing marriage with those boyfriends. What is marriage going to be worth to you now?

Don't answer that yet.

Girls in particular love having the sleepovers. You get to cuddle and watch movies and it's all very domestic, but after that first sleepover, then why not once more? What could it hurt? It's getting late. Plus you love cuddling in bed with him in the morning. How about only on weekends? Well, that's fun, but then maybe you should have a toothbrush at his place just in case, oh, and something to sleep in, and some stuff there to get ready for work. Ah, but now

American Idol is on every Tuesday and Wednesday. So how about just on those days then?

Now you two are almost living together after only two months! You drool on the pillow, he snores, you pee with the door open, and he leaves his underwear on the floor. You both shower together.

"We're so comfortable together!"

Guess what? Intimacy, *true intimac*y, takes a lifetime to perfect. You're doing all the married things, without the marriage. You've gleaped a good 20 years in relationship time (*Quantum Leap*: Google that one, best TV show ever. Shit, I might be thinking of *Out of This World*, when Evie freezes time. I'm confused, was her dad actually in the crystal? You think you've got daddy issues, at least your dad is on the same planet!)

Once Upon a Time...

A boy would have to convince the girl to allow him the opportunity to take her out for dinner. He would come ask her father, meet the mother and have her back home by nine. Her friends were the high court; no losers allowed near the queen. After all, she didn't want no scrubs! He was a proper gentleman and wouldn't dream of putting a penis- I mean hand- on her knee. Not yet anyway. It was too soon for all that.

They just weren't there yet.

Soon though they were "going steady." Kissing, some more kissing and some serious petting would occur. Maybe they'd have one or two dinners at the house with the whole family, but even that was pushing it. I mean they'd only been dating for six months now!

Eventually they'd be parked in a car, 2nd base here we come! God, drive-in movies are awesome. Well, one thing leads to another and they have "the sex"! Sadly though, he had to go off to war. She wrote him every single week. She was his perfect little bird 'til he strayed with an Asian girl (he's a guy, plus she showed him this thing called a "the 69"). They pulled through it though, and when he returned home from battle they made a pretty tiny baby together and had a beautiful white wedding. Before God and their families they promised to love, cherish and respect one another until death. Her dress cost thirty dollars. They pretended that she wasn't pregnant and had sex for the "first time" in a fancy schmancy hotel room. The honeymoon was simple and afterward, with their entire lives ahead of them, they moved into a modest house in the same town they'd grown up in. On that first night, while laying next to one another, as they both stared up at the imperfect cracks in the ceiling, wide eyed, too nervous to fall asleep, they wondered... though neither one spoke it aloud...

"What the fuck am I doing here?"
"Is that his underwear on the floor?"
"Is that her toothbrush on the sink?"

It would take them the rest of their lives to grow their relationship into something strong that couldn't be broken or grown tired of. A relationship with true intimacy is one that can only be created with true love, which can only come from time. There are no secrets or great mysteries here. It took love, patience, respect, kindness and understanding.

It wasn't easy.

What's amazing is that for some reason we think that it should be. While we all agree that we'd like to have that kind of love, we foolishly try to force the same outcome after only a few weeks of dating. It's that rush, that arrogance, of wanting the same results without putting in the hard work, which continues to leave wounded boy and broken girl. Listen, you'll never get the marriage that Disney, *The Notebook* or Taylor Swift told you about if you keep having these casual sleepovers. It creates a false sense of intimacy between two people who have put in little or no work at all. It feels like the real thing, looks like the real thing, and even seems to be growing into something special, but then it crashes down all around us, and we swear up and down that we'll be more careful the next time around. Of course old habits are hard to break. So we do it again, rush things again, get hurt again, feel fucking stupid again, blame the other person again, and then we wonder again, "What were we thinking?" Nostalgia is a tenacious little prick, and he works his way back into our hearts, just like Michael Jackson did. We're absolutely powerless, and in a drunken state of emotions we think we can cheat love AGAIN!

Look, if you're not sure how to break out of this fucked up cycle, when he asks you why you won't stay with him, you can say:

"Because we're just not there yet."

Is cuddling and then waking up in the morning next to someone nuzzled in your arms wonderful? Of course it is. Is it going to be hard to sleep alone? Yes! But aren't you finally ready to have a real relationship?

You always have a choice. If you're young right now and want to just keep messing around, dating different people, hooking up, giving blowjobs... believe me, I get it. Enjoy herpes. I heard it's awesome!

To be fair though, I see the allure. Remember, I was the king of that lifestyle. Sometimes it's great. But sometimes it's just awful. I can tell you this much, you can't play house and expect it to turn into a committed, healthy relationship. It's like showing up to a job every day for five years, doing the least amount of work to get by, and then wondering why you're not the boss yet.

If you're really ready to build something that will last a lifetime and not just until your first divorce, then you'll have to put the time into it. You can't build a house in a month and expect it to last twenty years unless, of course, you have Ty Pennington (good luck paying the fucking taxes on it, though). You also can't work out once every two weeks and still expect to have a banging body! I'm all out of analogies. You either get it or you don't.

There, I've said my piece...

I need a fucking drink, and a strong one. How about you? I thought that you might! How about we meet back here tomorrow.

Tomorrow...

The analogies got me thinking, one of the best things that you can do is to go on more dates. You'll get better at it each time you do. I think that you should go on as many dates as you can tolerate. The more you do something, the better you'll get at it. Painting, making friendship bracelets, running, fucking, needle work... it all takes tons of practice.

Just like dating.

How else will you know what to look for? What you like in a guy? What you don't like? You would think the answer is as simple as,

"I don't know, I *just* know!"

It's true, some girls know what they like and don't like from their limited past experiences, and that is a problem.

I had this conversation with a guy I used to work with:

> He said, "I really liked this girl who I was with, but the deal breaker for me, was that she wouldn't ever let me go down on her. She said she didn't care for it, so I told her, 'Well you've never let me even try it!' And she said, 'Well that's because when I've done it before, I didn't really like it!'"

Any girl reading this now who has ever had it done properly for her is thinking the same thing, "She has no idea

what she's missing out on. Way better than the Rabbit!!!"
(Google that.)

Girls have a bad habit of comparing the new guys to
people from their past. Past boyfriends, past lovers, fathers
and crushes. This poor guy was not able to satisfy his girl
because some lover from her past didn't know his way
around? That doesn't make any sense to me. You can't be
afraid to start a new chapter. Go on dates, meet boys. Some
will be nothing like your ex. Some will be even better than
him and some will remind you of him to an exact tee. Just be
open to something new.
Why not? It's not forever, it's lunch. I like that. That
could be my next book title. (Note to self, trademark that
title.)
Besides, it doesn't have to be this whole big thing.
Just go out a few times with him. It can be as simple as a cup
of coffee or a drink. You can't keep putting so much pressure on a single date. You can't just sit there quietly, really
offering nothing to the date, and hope that it's going to turn
into something. You also can't have your guard up, ready to
bail out, as soon as he starts to annoy you.
You're supposed to be getting to know one other.
All you should be "feeling" right now is hungry for lunch.
All this carrying on and worrying about what he's really
thinking or being upset, wondering why he hasn't called
you? He's just a boy you've had lunch with two times, why
do you even give a damn what he thinks anyway? You say
you don't care, but you clearly do, why?

Well let me ask you this…

Have you hooked up with him yet?

You did?!

Ok, well you didn't stay the night though, right?

Damn, you did?

Ok, shit, well then please tell me you didn't hook up with him again in the morning?

Fuck. Well no wonder why you care so much. Read the last section again, I think you may have missed some of it.

Three

Wing Girls...

What exactly is a wing girl? Well, you know when you're out drinking and you meet a guy that's there with his best buddies? There's always at least one guy in the bunch who's playing the whole, "my boy's way smart" role. That's his wingman! Guys don't leave home without them. A wingman's main job is to play a supporting role for his bro. Think Ben Affleck to Matt Damon, or Lance Armstrong to Matthew McConaughey or Bert to Ernie (actually, that last one might not really work too well). Either way it's basically a guy friend who's there to help make sure his bro looks his absolute best. Quick with a joke or to light up your smoke, ready to break the silence, and always down to bail at a moment's notice.

Girls, you have them too. Only yours are known as professional cock blocks. The main difference is this:

A wingman is a helping role. A wing girl, on the other hand, plays a judging role. She is there to suck and to condemn.

Nothing is worse for a guy than having the wing girl of the new girl that he's into, making him feel like he's auditioning for the role of a lifetime.

"If this all goes well tonight, you could be with MY friend. Forever."

Damn it, I knew I should have worn my Ed Hardy shoes and not just the shirt!

Really?

Alright my public service announcement is coming up in 3... 2... 1...

Look, nobody should be wearing that stuff, not anymore. It's *way* past done, unless maybe you're Nick Hogan. Thanks to Ed Hardy and Affliction now every other boy has a shirt on with a million crazy colors and sparkles on it, and might I add, ninety less dollars in his pocket to take you out to dinner or to put gas into his rad Fast and the Furious style Honda Civic. It's almost like if South Beach had intercourse with a Bedazzler and then their baby puked all over the Buckle, Macy's and Express. Even dress shirts aren't safe anymore. The worst part is that it didn't only stay down in

Miami. We went out the other night in Charlotte, and this guy had on the Ed Hardy trucker hat, paired with the Ed Hardy shirt, which he had tucked in to show off his Ed Hardy belt, topped off with his Ed Hardy jeans and, yes, the fucking shoes to match it all! I almost took a picture.

My wingman was ready though and chimed in with a little joke- one of his many jobs as a wingman.

Wingman: "Dude, either that guy really likes him some Ed Hardy, or THAT IS Ed Hardy!"

My date: "Hee hee hee, that's funny!"

-We ordered another drink-

Nice work wingman, keeping it light!

So getting back to wing girls. They come in all different shapes and sizes, and some are much worse for you than others, believe me. So how do you tell which one you have, or which of them is the best to keep around? All great questions. No worries darling, we're about to go over it all. We've given them nicknames to make it easier. So let's get started...

The Crazy Interrogation Wing Girl

I'm out for drinks meeting the new girl I like, (that's you) and you've invited along your best girlfriend, the one who you promised I'll love and just have to meet.

> "Carrie is the best, she is fucking hilarious, and you'll love her! I promise!"

Most of the time this seems simple enough. I do have to meet your friends sooner or later, right? Everything is going swell, your girlfriend even seems to be taking a genuine liking to me. Which is always a good thing because every guy knows that he can't get the girl if her girlfriends think he's lame. So I'm trying extra hard to get your friend to think I'm perfect for you. I'm being funny, buying the drinks and your girl even squealed out loud,

> "OMG, Shut up, you're soooo bad. *He is so bad!*"

before punching me playfully in the arm. Everything seems to be going great until you stand up and utter those five terrifying words:

> "I'm going to the bathroom."

So you start to walk away from the table, and your friend stays put? Wait a minute, that doesn't seem right. Everything I've learned about girls so far has taught me that you go to the bathroom in pairs. Why hasn't she gotten up yet to follow you? I feel my mouth start to go dry; I feel like a lost child in a department store. Isn't Mom coming back? I start to get nervous and then as soon as you're safely out of our earshot I hear your friend say to me,

"Listen, you know she just got of a very serious relationship, he cheated on her, it was awful."

"Are you a player? I heard you hook up with a lot of girls, which is not a good thing because I think she's really falling for you."

"I hope you know I've never seen her like this before with a guy, I can tell that she really likes you, she says you two get along really well... and it's crazy, she never says stuff like that!"

"Hey, have you ever cheated on a girlfriend? Well would you ever?"

Think quickly D! Damn, where is my fucking Twix bar? I need a moment...

"No! I haven't. Hold on a second, do you mean would I cheat right now, like with you? No, I wouldn't cheat. B. The answer is B, right? Can I phone a friend?"

And finally...

"You'd better not tell her anything that I've said, because I'll deny all of it!"

It's right about this time that you come bopping around the corner, smiling, excited to be back. I'm sitting there still stunned, but your girlfriend quickly chimes in with something sweet like,

"You were right, he *is* really funny!"

This is me, sitting here, completely freaked out. I am Jack's complete sense of confusion.

What the hell just happened? I was just blindsided by your friend! I'm still getting to know you, we're having drinks, flirting a bit, things seemed to be going great, and the very second you get up and leave the table, your girlfriend turns into a conversational wizard! I think she was inside of my head. Check my nose, is it bleeding? So many questions. Who is your friend anyway? Is she a cop? Wait a minute, how old are you? I might as well have been tied up to a chair. It was almost as bad as having Chris Hanson walk in on our date...

Chris Hanson: Hi I'm Chris Hanson with Dateline's *To Catch a Guy to Marry*. Why don't you take a seat and tell me what you're doing here.

Me: Um, well, I was... see, we're just friends, she messaged me on Facebook and she said we should have a drink and...

Chris Hanson: And you thought it would be okay to come have drinks without answering some questions about your past? What were you thinking?

Me: I just thought it would be a chill night, maybe a few laughs and, I don't know, maybe a kiss goo...

Chris Hanson: A kiss goodnight? I thought you wanted to get to know her. Let me ask you this, do you kiss a lot of girls at bars?

Me: I have, I mean sometimes, but I swear I didn't think anything would happen tonight.

Chris Hanson: You didn't think anything was going to happen? Well, we found a condom and mint gum in your car. Can you explain that?

Me: Um, yeah. They're not mine?

Chris Hanson: Well, we also have your Facebook transcripts, I'm going to read them to you: 'Beth... What's up? We should grab a drink this week, I know a great spot to get an apple martini, and you should bring Carrie. It should be fun, can't wait to see you... I still need to get that kiss we talked about... and by the way, your body is banging.'

Me: Um...

Chris Hanson: These are your words, right? Don't you think it's a bit inappropriate to come here and try to fool around with her before you even know what her favorite color is?

Me: I know, I know. Look, you're not going to tell my wife, right?

Chris Hanson: (Shaking his head disgustedly) You're free to go.

All right, so maybe it's not always quite that bad. Girls do invite their Chris Hanson interrogators out for drinks way too often though. It's a no win situation for either party and it will push your guy away fast. The crazy part is that whenever I try to tell girls that this stuff actually happens when they're away in the bathroom, they never believe me and act shocked- amazed even- that girls would behave like this.

> "I don't know any girls like that!"
> "She sounds like a crazy bitch!"

I KNOW! That's what's so messed up, these are "your" friends! Which means that you must be doing the exact same thing for them! No matter what I say though, girls will never come clean or admit to it. The closest I've ever gotten was:

> "Yeah, maybe she is a little forward sometimes, I mean I've done it too, but I was just kidding."

Look, this stuff does go on, and it is a huge red flag. It's not cool or protective. It's plain crazy. And when it happens, we start inspecting you for cracks in the foundation. Guys know that crazy girls don't fall far from the crazy tree.

The Old G Wing Girl

This is the girlfriend who is ride or die. She has been around the longest and is the girlfriend who will stick with you through thick and thin. If your guy can't win her over, he will never have a shot. She knows you better than anyone else does and holds the most secrets about you too! She has your back no matter what goes down and would be willing to cut almost anyone if it ever came to that. And if you're a guy reading this, remember one thing, the Old G's hate, I repeat, HATE, kiss-asses. So don't even try, because she won't buy it!

The Wasted Face Wing Girl

This is your girlfriend who loves taking shots and thinks Jägermeister is awesome. She has various tricks up her skirt and has probably puked on her cat once or twice before. Just like Benjamin Button, she can become childlike right before your very eyes. It's almost like bringing a puppy or a baby out to drink with you. It's lots of work. She always seems to be in the way or causing a scene.

> "I have to take my friend home, she's wasted, I'm sorry!"

We hate this one! If your wing girl drinks way too much she can ruin the whole evening for us. She's falling asleep at the table or puking in the bathroom. Really? Who are these friends of yours?

The wasted face wing girl is the first one to fall down and the first one to need help walking. She is never able to make it to her own bed, and is often known as "the crier." After just two drinks and one shot, the tears start flowing. Often, she will ruin common household items like lamps, clocks, plants and end tables. She should never be left alone near open windows either.

Dealing with drunken girls is actually a lot like chatting with two year olds.

"Hey where's your shoe, how did you lose a shoe? No, it's time to go home, you have five more minutes, ok? No, I'm not mad at you, everyone loves you. Ok, now say bye-bye..."

The Married Wing Girl

She is boring, only comes around once in a blue moon, and talks about babies, Elmo, and how amazing being a mom is. Basically she shits on everyone else's relationships. Beware because sometimes she is really just using you to feel young again. Married people are like super old people who don't have sex anymore. They really should just have their own special bars and restaurants.

The Dirty Wing Girl

This is your most skanky girlfriend. Most guys are protective of girls by nature. We all have sisters, cousins, mommies and nieces. We feel like we have to play the big brother to all women. A protector of sorts, especially when they're in harm's way. If we're running around trying to save your dirty wing girl from having to take yet another morning after pill, we aren't really focusing on you. It's safe to say that we will most likely not be going out again.

"I've never seen her act like this, it's really not like her."

"She's going through a really bad break up, sorry."

"She's just trying to get over her ex, again."

No, she's just a dirty wing girl.

She's also the one who has hooked up with everybody's ex, but swears up and down that:

> "It happened way before you ever dated him!"

> "It was nothing, just kissing."

> "I don't even look at him like that... anymore."

Listen she is major trouble for your relationship, so ditch her.

The Normal One Wing Girl

She scares us the most. Why aren't there more of her type around? Something's not right. Something is definitely up with this one.

The Mom Wing Girl

This is your girlfriend who talks you up like you're her very own daughter. She tells you which boys to like and what to wear. She has a fucking opinion about everything. She often talks about you like you're not even standing there in the room. This is a turn off for your guy, and it doesn't make you look good. Besides, you wouldn't let her do that to you at your work or at your school would you?

"Sir, Tara has really been working super hard on the proposal for the Lyell account. She stayed late three nights this week!"

"Professor, Kimberly is willing to do extra credit. She loves political science, but is having a hard time with the essays."

That's some pretty annoying stuff. So why let her do that with the new guy you're dating? I don't need your girlfriend's opinion to decide whether or not I like you. The wing girl mom's most annoying trait though, is telling stories from your past ...

Mom W.G: You know, Shelby and I went to the same high school together, and we both used to cheer, the varsity squad, of course. We learned how to do back hand springs in my front yard, so after cheer practice we'd watch *Saved by the Bell* and I had a crush on Zack, and Amber had one on Slater, and we both couldn't stand Kelly, remember? Because she reminded us of this one girl from JV cheer, her name wasn't Kelly, but she kind of looked like her, except way more skanky, and then she was voted homecoming queen, it was so rigged though, Amber do you remember that!?

Amber: I know she was such a bitch! Do you remember she was dating that guy, Eric...

Both Girls: Michaels!

Amber: OMG, he was so out of her league! So Eric was this guy at our high school who kind of looked like a young Matthew Macana... blah blah blah blah blah blah blah blah blah blah blah blah blah blah blah blah blah blah blah blah blah blah blah blah blah blah blah blah blah blah blah blah blah blah blah blah blah...

Both: Blah blah...

Blah blah blah blah blah blah blah blah blah blah blah blah blah blah blah blah blah blah blah blah blah blah blah blah bla it was so funny, Amber remember you laughed so hard a little pee came out!!

Amber: Isn't that crazy?

Amber: Baby? Baby, were you even listening to us?

Me: Whoa, I'm sorry, I zoned out. I tried to listen; I heard everything right up until you said 'you know?' But then I realized I didn't really give a fuck, I'm sorry that was rude of me, ok tell me more... Did you have an awesome time? Did you drink awesome shooters, listen to awesome music, and then just sit around and soak up in each other's awesomeness? (*Mean Girls*). I didn't realize that you were so 'fetch' in high school, baby please tell me more exciting stories.

Believe me, your date doesn't care even a little bit who you were, or what you were doing in high school, or how awesome it all was. He doesn't care about what amazing things happened. Even if you graduated two months ago, it's still not relevant to him. Maybe you were the homecoming queen or rescued a little blue kid from a pool. I would love to hear all about it, but I want to hear about it from you! Not from your agent. Bottom line is this, your wing girl does not need to try and sell you to me, or speak for you.

The Love Crack Head Wing Girl

This is your girlfriend that's always in love with some boy who's fricking amazing! Yes, she says "fricking." She somehow is convinced several times a year that she's truly in love, and this time, it's for real! She is in love with falling in love, that's all it really is. She has seen *The Notebook* maybe a hundred times, and she also thinks that Carrie Bradshaw is a real person. When Hollywood couples split up, she cries. But she also cried at the end of *Twilight*, so there's that I guess? Look, she's a sweet girl and harmless really. Just make sure you tell her that you're very happy for her and she'll be just fine. The most important thing to remember when dealing with this particular wing girl is to nod "yes" a lot! She will talk and talk and talk, so nodding yes now and

again will help you to get through it. Also if you want to
throw in an "I know!" "Shut up, really?" and "Uh huh..."
that can't hurt either!

The Denial Queen Wing Girl

She is in the worst relationship ever and will never listen or
take advice; she has to learn her lessons the hard way. Even
though everyone knows that he cheats on her and sucks at
life, she won't hear it. Don't waste too much time on her,
you could be making out right now with your man instead of
spending more time going through her dumb bullshit again.

The Healthy Wing Girl

This is your girlfriend who's, um, "healthy." She's not as hot
as some of your other friends, and she doesn't really dance
as much. She always seems to be saving somebody a seat.
Ok look, I'm talking about your fat friend. I know it's not a
very nice thing to say, and I know that some "healthy" people will be reading this book. I'm not trying to hurt anybody's feelings, what I'm trying to say is that being a fat,
happy wing girl is a great thing, but being a fat, hateful wing
girl, isn't. Look, every girl has a fat friend, and even if
you're a bit fat yourself, you still have an even fatter friend
around. Most times though, it's the fat friend with the click
of skinnier girls. We call them the "Blondetourage," and
every Blondetourage has its very own Turtle.

It's as if they keep one fat friend around to help
themselves avoid eating seconds, (skinny little bitches) or to
make sure they'll have a designated driver at the end of the
night. I don't blame her for being pissed off either. I get it. I

would be, too. However, this is still one of the worst possible wing girls you can have around, and it's mostly because she's almost always hateful and bitter, and quite honestly she probably hates you. I haven't ever met the happy one yet. I have met tons of bitter, angry ones though, and it's never a good scene. If you let her loose to wander around, she'll make the whole night miserable for you and your date, so it's really best to set her loose somewhere else to frolic around on her own. Don't say it, you're going to make me say it, aren't you? Fuck it, I guess we've come this far together.

If the above rings true for you, it's time to do the humane thing and...

Free Willy.

The Trustworthy Wing Girl

This is the girlfriend who is trust... ah, who am I kidding...

The Ego-Maniac Wing Girl

This is your girlfriend who thinks she's a nine, but she's actually a six and a half. She is convinced that everyone is trying to fuck her, and is always reminding you of all the "hot" guys who, in fact, have. She is the first one to upload Facebook photos the next morning, and she's always complaining to you about all the boys who won't stop text-ing her (even though she is the first to text them). All she really wants is just a nice guy. Please! She's cute for sure, but her ego is a big problem. She has this sick need to know that every guy would fuck her, even your guy! She's a big fan of status symbols, a true star fucker for sure. Don't be surprised if a baseball player knocks her up.

The Work Wing Girl

This is the girlfriend from work who you have lunch with, send forwarded emails to, and Facebook chat with all day long, even though she sits only three feet away from you. You share a common hatred for your boss, and you both think the guy who sits three cubes down is kind of creepy, but sort of sexy in a way. She is your office BFF. Sometimes you go out after work together for a drink, and when she has a dentist or doctor's appointment, you miss her terribly all day long.

The work wing girl is a very common one because naturally it's nice to have a good friend at work. You know, someone to gossip with you about work drama. Somebody who's close to you and who really "gets" what you go through all day long. The downside of having her act as your best wing girl is that you two often slip into work talk when you're out. I'll tell you why this is an awful habit. See, when a guy agrees to be out with you and your friends, he's there to make you happy and he may even be looking forward to getting to know your friends a bit better. Sitting at a table having a few drinks, all while you and your work girls chat it up about the latest office drama, well, that's about as much fun for us as going to the DMV. Even though we have to do it, we would rather be anywhere else. And why?

1. We don't have a clue what you're talking about.
2. We don't work there.
3. We don't really care about what goes on at your work.

I know it's a hard thing not to do. Guys do it all the time and are often much worse about it. It's no better when they do it, either. Here's the thing. Almost all of this book can go both ways. The same stuff that girls do that makes guys crazy is also the stuff that makes us not want to be friends with other guys. To be honest, I hate it when my guy friends talk about work. I also hate when they get so drunk that I have to babysit them. See, how a guy picks his friends is actually a huge piece of the puzzle to what he's looking for in a girl. You have to be his friend too, right? So keep your eyes peeled, try and see why he has the friends he has. You may be able to learn some things.

Does this mean that you should try to play sports, drink whiskey and smoke cigars because that's what he likes his friends to do? No, dig a bit deeper dear. What I'm saying is this: I love girls, and the ones I love to go out with are always super girly. I love when they hate bugs, smell pretty, wear cute shoes, need help putting shit together, match their nail polish to their outfits, and so on. I always pick that type, but the ones that I actually date are the ones that remind me of my guy friends. Now the best guy friends I have, and the only ones who I keep around, have a few simple requirements...

1. Be honest.
2. Be sincere.
3. Be on my side.
4. Be in a good mood.
5. Be able to accept me for who I am.

Guy friends or girl friends, that's how I pick them, that's all I need. Guys aren't simple. That's a myth. We're simply looking for the least amount of work. Guys don't keep friends around who require a lot of work, and we feel the same way when it comes to our women. We will still date you, sleep with you, even marry you, but if you want us to be a good man, a happy man, and only your man, the answers lie above. You follow those five steps and you will have mastered men. It's a tall order, but it can be done, or so I've heard.

What June Carter Taught Us...

Think about sweet June Carter, the poster girl for true love in country music. It wasn't easy though. I'm sure she could have had a much easier time with a different man. Less work and less heartache. A man who would never break her heart or take her for granted. She didn't want that though, she wanted Johnny, and if she wanted Johnny Cash, she had to love him for being who he was and just hope for the best. Nagging him to death wasn't going to make him act better or be different, but loving him with those five rules would.

Watch the movie again and see the difference between his first wife Vivian and June. In reality, the whole story is pretty messed up, and it really speaks volumes for how girls view love. Vivian had every right in the world to be upset and angry. She was being cheated on and left behind with four children to raise by herself. Johnny and June became the king and queen of country music and rode off into the sunset in a storybook romance.

This was the story that moved women everywhere? I remember when *Walk the Line* came out. All the girls were gushing over how romantic it was! Johnny and June.

"I want a love like that!"

It seems that with girls it's always okay as long as it's not happening to them or to their friends. June got her man, well, yay for her! Vivian lost her family? That's considered romantic? No wonder love is so confusing.

Vivian screamed, cried, and demanded that he be better and that things be different; after all, she deserved that. It shows though that sometimes you can't win, no matter what, even if you're right. So you have to decide for yourself. You can't just wish things to be different, or for them to be better. You have to be prepared to be happy with what you have, even if it never changes. June wanted

Johnny, despite the drugs, women, cheating and all. That was the key to their happiness. That's why it worked. Vivian wanted what any normal person would want, a father for her children, a husband for herself and all of the other things she was promised at their wedding. The problem was all those things she wanted, he wasn't, and never would be. You can't change a man. You can get him to act changed, but you can't change him. Not even if you're June Carter.

So back to the rest of the wing girls…

The Bitch Wing Girl

This is the girlfriend who starts fights and feuds with everyone and says really mean things. She sucks, but you need to have one to complete the whole set, so suck it up.

The Wing Girl Hottie

This is one of my favorite ones. I like to refer to her as, "The smoking hot with the crazy-sick body wing girl." If you're hanging out with a new guy, and you think that you may be starting to really like him, never bring out the wing girl hottie! It's got nothing to do with trusting him, or trusting her, this one is all about you. If you've ever thought to yourself, "Hey I think my girlfriend is hotter and cooler than me," well, she probably is. And that shouldn't matter to you anyway because chances are she's not your date's type at all. It's really about how you act and talk around her. It shows your guy that you think she would be the better choice for him. I've never understood why girls bring their friend who they truly feel is their competition out with them and their man. We've all been there before; every girl has a friend who's just as hot and just as cool as she is. It's called life, but if you bring her, how come *we* get in trouble?

If you're covered up and your wing girl hottie is busting out of her top, guess where I'm trying my hardest not to look, and I will look, and it's not *my* fault because *you* brought *her* and *she* brought *them*. It's not just about being hot, either. It's about having self-confidence. If you're insecure, and your wing girl hottie is really funny and outgoing, it's going to make you seem that much more insecure. When I'm dating a girl, I can always tell which one of her friends she secretly wants to be like. Or which one she thinks I'd be into. It's strange. We're there because we like you, but even knowing this, girls will still dangle their best friend in front of us and ask questions like…

"Don't you think she's really hot?"

"Her body is rocking, right?"

"Do you wish I was into sports like her?"

"I could see you two together, she has the same sense of humor."

"I think she is way more your type than I am."

If I'm out with you, I'm not there to be nice or out of pity. I'm there because I'm into you. No one compares to you at this moment in time. I'm excited to be around you and think that you're amazing.

Now, it's right about this time you pull me from love land to remind me that there are so many other girls out there, your hot friend included, who may be better for me than you. Don't do this. It's weird.

Well, that's about it, I think we've covered them all. At this point, you might be wondering who's your best wing girl? There is no simple answer. And as you can see, there are many types to choose from. Just be careful about who you surround yourself with, and more importantly, be careful which friends you bring around your new boy. Don't let a "friend" that you don't truly care about, ruin a great thing for you. You will be judged by the friends you keep… sorry.

Four

Cocktails

Going out for drinks together is always where the excitement starts. You think you like the new guy you've been seeing? Well, have you seen him wasted face yet? I would recommend you wait until after you've see him have "the evil drink" before making your final purchase. For most of us, drinking is a constant cast member in our lives. It's everywhere. Every time we go out to be social, Uncle Jack and Aunt Stoli are there to chaperone us.

You go out for dinner, you drink.
You go to the ball game, you drink.
You play kickball, you drink.
You go to a baby shower, you drink.
You go to a wedding, you drink.

It's almost unavoidable, it's become a part of our everyday adult lives, or maybe it always has been. Even Jesus got his drink on (as the kids would say) and if you don't drink, well I'll let Christian Bale take this one...

"Oh, good for you!"

Now, for the rest of us here in adult world, alcohol is a major player in our social scene. Since we can't avoid it, it's best we talk about how to control the beast.

I would never tell you not to drink. I love drinking. In fact, to be honest with you, I'm drinking right now while I'm writing this. I'm in Milwaukee, sitting at a place called McGillycuddy's. My drink of choice for this summer is gin and lemonade. Last summer it was amaretto sours, don't ask! Anyhow, most days I come out to the patio here, have myself a few drinks, and work on this fucking book. I love drinking. It's a part of my everyday life. I'm far from alone on this. Milwaukee itself is known for its drinking lifestyle. They have more bars per capita than most major cities could dream of, so maybe that's to blame for my vice. Neither of my parents drink, but my brother has been in the alcohol business for almost his entire adult career. He has represented them all: vodka, whiskey, rum, gin, you name it. We're only about four years apart, so when I was seventeen, he was? Anyone? Anyone? Bueller? Bueller? Twenty-one years old. That's right. Good work.

I had a fake ID (well actually my brother's ID) when I was seventeen. I was living every high school kid's fantasy, but the Alanis Morissette part was that I didn't really drink. One, I had a girlfriend who couldn't drink, and two, I was nervous about getting caught. Still, I needed that ID because I played in three bands, and since they already thought I was twenty-one, I was stuck pretending. I would drink a beer after our shows, but that was really it.

Now my girlfriend was older than I was, so when she went off to college in Madison, Wisconsin, I finally understood what all this drinking fuss was about.

I went to Madison with her on move-in weekend. She was moving into one of the dorms. I was still in high school though, so I had to be back at home on Sunday night. What in the world were my parents thinking? That weekend, I got to see real college drinking for the first time in my life.

UW-Madison has over 40,000 students, and this was probably their biggest party weekend of the year. I was in *way* over my head. Playing the role of the quiet, tag-along boyfriend, I followed her and her new girlfriends, and watched in complete whore, I mean horror, as they became "real college girls." I was completely unprepared for my crash course in college life.

We wandered around for what seemed like all day, and then at night we'd go to these parties, returning back to the dorms to sleep. I had enough sense not to get too wasted face. I sipped on my beer, or whatever was in my red cup, but I never got close to being drunk. I figured this wouldn't be the best place to learn my tolerance- I still had my twenties for that. Instead, I hung out with the girls and... watched.

At night in the dorms is where my real education took place. Jell-O shots in this room, something green in that one, pretty girls bouncing around everywhere!

I was staying with my girlfriend in her dorm room, which was on the girl's side of the building. Her parents probably figured they were being responsible by having her live in the dorm which separated the boys and girls by a stairwell and an elevator. Well, I saw more naked people that weekend than I'd seen in my previous sixteen years of life. People were running up and down the halls, to and from the showers, some in their underwear, some wrapped in tiny towels. Not to mention the random hooking up that was taking place, all happening to the romantic backbeats of Eminem and Dave Matthews Band.

It seemed to me like the girls were having a blast. They were screaming, laughing, running, falling, hugging and kissing. Everyone was hammered. It was absolutely the very last place that you'd ever want your girlfriend to be, but what could I do about it?

So we finally made it to bed. She was more drunk than I'd ever seen her before. I was sober and annoyed. She seemed to want sex really bad, which was something that we'd done before, but now her roommate was sleeping right above us! In high school she'd be shy about me kissing me in the hallway, and now she wanted to have sex with someone else in the same room? I'd somehow managed to go no further than fooling around before she gave up on the idea, and passed out. She tasted like Jägermeister and peppermint schnapps… fucking freshmen.

In the morning her roommate got up first, changed her clothes in plain view, whispered "bye" to us, and left. This college stuff was crazy yo. High school girls were never like this. Even ones who wore bikinis on the band trip in Florida all seemed really nervous about showing any skin. They'd even wrap towels around their waists. Now though girls were changing their clothes in plain view?

Just as I was laying there, realizing my new lot in life, the door swung open and her girlfriend Ricki came in. She was with some other girls and she was sobbing. I couldn't get up though, I wasn't dressed all the way. I froze. It didn't seem to matter though that I was there, I might as well have been invisible. The girls started consoling Ricki, assuring her that it couldn't be that bad! She seemed really upset. What could have possibly happened? She seemed so happy and carefree just a few hours ago.

-Ricki sits down on the couch, still sobbing-

My Girl: Calm down, it's gonna be okay Ricki, what happened honey?

Ricki: I had way too much to drink last night and I ended up in Trent's room!

Girls: It's okay... what did he do, did he hurt you?

Ricki: No, we were fooling around (sniffle, sniffle) and one thing just led to another, and I... I... I gave him a blowjob!

Girls: Come here honey. It's ok, it happens... look, you didn't know what you were doing, you were wasted, right? He's an asshole!

Ricki: I feel so bad (more wailing) about my boyfriend...

Girls: You don't have to tell him, just don't do it again. You were drunk. It's not like you meant to do it.

Now I was really confused. She has a fucking boyfriend? And nobody in the entire room, except for me, thinks that maybe she should tell him? Should I raise my hand?

Ricki: I love my boyfriend, I would never cheat on him. I didn't mean to get that drunk, I barely even remember it.

Girls: Well that's too bad because now we'll never know if Trent has a big dick or not...

-Girls laughing-

Girls: We all know that you love your boyfriend, at least Trent's hot, just be glad it wasn't with his fat friend Mike!

Ricki: Thanks guys (sniffle) I think it was pretty big, I mean I remember a little bit (giggles) I really just don't wanna see him today.

Girls: Don't worry, we're all here for you honey.

-End Scene-

Are you fucking kidding me? I wasn't really sure what to think. I knew I needed clothes and an exit. Was this a typical thing? My girlfriend didn't say much about it, but I was super sketched out, and I felt really bad for Ricki's boyfriend. I think my thought at the time was, "Well she's not my girlfriend to be worrying about, so what could I do?" If the same thing were to happen now though? I'd Facebook that dude faster than Jessica Simpson's movies go to DVD.

The weekend ended, and I went back to high school land. I felt like E.T., all out of place and wobbly around the high school girls. I was scared for what they'd all eventually become. I wanted to go home. I'd been to the other world and back again, and I'd never be the same. I would visit her on the weekends, and every time, just like clockwork, we'd have a new pretty girl crying her eyes out, torn up about something she had done and hadn't really meant to do. The details were always hazy, but one thing was guaranteed… she was tricked!

"I don't really remember what happened last night!"

"Guys suck, they shouldn't let us get that drunk."

"All they care about is sex, they try to get us wasted."

"I'm not sure if we had sex or not."

"I mean, I don't even remember drinking that much! Maybe there was something in my cup?"

Um, yeah… it's called Tequila.

I was still confused, I knew a couple of girls in high school, that people had said did things like this, but they were known as sluts, whores, or scallywags (great word by the way), and there were only a few of them, mostly because nobody wanted to be friends with those types of girls. It was a different story in college land though, it seemed that every other girl had a story, which included…

"I was so wasted, I don't remember what happened."

"I think we used a condom, but I'm not really sure."

"Don't let me go over to his room tonight, no matter how drunk I get!"

"You only get to be hot and young once, other girls are way worse than me. This is what happens in college, whoo hoo!"

So it seemed to me like the real problem was that college cocktails were stronger maybe? That's all I could come up with because girls, it seemed, were remembering very little about their nights and kept doing things that they never meant to do, and it was happening to them over and over again!

Of course I know much better now. See back then I was young and sweet. I truly believed in "honest mistakes." I was sure that sweet girls were being tricked by the masses. I mean look, the shiny red cups? Come on! How about the pretty, yummy, Jell-O shots? As far as I could see, it was all a big set up!

A lot of time has passed, and I've been drunk in more bars, in more cities, than maybe anybody else that I know. I've spent almost ten years, all of my twenties, traveling around for work. I have seen it all as far as drunken girl science goes. I can tell you, without any hesitation, that girls pull this move everywhere. It's not just a young girl thing either; they over-serve themselves, knowing full well that it's going to end, just like it did the last time. The blame is always placed on everyone except the person who actually held the glass, and when it goes to trial in the morning, the well-prepped defendant is ready with her fail-safe opening statement...

"I don't remember (batting eyelashes)... what happened last night?"

Maybe you really, truly don't remember. Is that cool though? Why would you want to be like that with some random guy? I really shouldn't have to keep saying this, but I

will if it will help calm you down. *I know that guys do it too!*
All right? But you shouldn't date those guys! Really, don't
do it. Okay then, let's move on. I want to go over some other
things so that if you are out drinking with him, you won't
remind him of a "Ricki."

Know Your Limits...

Know your limits, and know them well. Maybe you have an evil drink? The evil drink is the one that makes you evil after just two of them. Whatever your "evil drink" is, steer clear of it if you're out on a date. If you know that Jamo will get you wasted face like no other, save it for your girls' night out. If you can't handle shooting Jack (pussy), how about don't order it. And before I forget, martinis are for the pros. The girls on *Sex and the City* can put down four of them in under an hour! Um, that's because it's a fucking TV show! In real life, you become the girl who walks around the bar like a preschooler. Missing a shoe, dropping things, stumbling into tables, and going up to strangers while they're trying to eat. And I have to walk behind you and clean up your mess...

Table: Well hello! What a pretty dress! And how old are you?

You: 23, I'm 23! And I just had a birthday, this is my dress, and this is Katie's purse, she let me use it, do you like cats?

Table: Well, it's a lovely purse, sure cats are nice?

You: I have a cat named Paris!

-You walk (stumble) away from the table-

Me: I'm so sorry.

Table: It's okay, is it her birthday?

Me: Um no, just a Tuesday.

Very cute, can we please leave right now and go look for rings! Of course, we can't forget to mention margaritas. Do I really need to even explain that one? Look, I love to drink 44 North and Red Bull. I also know that I can only handle maybe four of them because after that I get... well, it doesn't really matter how I get because you will never see me like that. You know why? Because I would never do it on a date! It's ok to get wasted face with your girlfriends, or with a guy that's just a friend, but not with the new guy you're dating.

> "You hook up with a boyfriend, you don't turn your hookups into them!"

You'll likely end up meeting for the first time at a place serving the sweet poison. You can go ahead and have a few drinks with him, but don't go overboard. Getting a baby buzz is great, and it's a good test to see what kind of guy you're dealing with. Buzzed girls are cute, wasted face girls on the other hand, not so much. If he thinks it's cute when you can barely walk or keep your eyes open, he's a question mark, I promise. Don't date guys who try to get you wasted. It's not a good place to start any relationship. A good rule for the beginning is this:

> Don't get any drunker with your date than you would get in front of his parents if they were sitting there at the table with you.

Guys take mental notes from the very beginning. We watch and we learn. We try and see if you're better suited for a hook up, or as a girlfriend. You can't be both. So we have to assign you a role. It's something that we pride ourselves on. We can spot random hook up girls before they even get out their fake ID's. We know all the signs, and if the signs are unclear, we'll wait around for you to have your 4th or 5th drink before we'll make the call.

What are all these signs, you ask? Listen, I can't tell you. No, I really can't, it's guy code and I'm sworn to protect it, we all are actually. It happens right after we get circumcised. They do the snip, and then they say…

> "You've got a grown up penis now, I know you were just born, but we need to prepare you for what lies ahead. Here are the ways you can tell if a bar girl will be better for a hookup or for a girlfriend…"

-Doctor explains it all to me. I am silent and take it all in-

> "Now nod if you understand me. Ok, just blink then. Good, now you can never tell another girl what I've just told you, they're all sisters buddy, so be careful. I think you're going to make it…"

No really though, I can't tell you. I'll be happy to give you a hint though if you'd like. It all comes down to this: how far out of control do you get when you're drunk? Some people get quiet, and some people get pregnant. Some people like to fight, and some people just want to fuck. You might be a really sweet girl, but when you take that forth shot of Jack, you get crazy jealous, and even though you trust him completely, you've now become convinced that he's checking out all the waitresses. People change when they drink. All of us do. Some change for the worse and some really for the best. Is it a bad thing?

Well, it all depends on what you're looking for. If it's all about having fun and hooking up, then go for it. However, if you really want to be in a relationship and date somebody, then we need to talk! Mixing dating and drinking can be the fastest way to have your relationship go absolutely nowhere. Your relationship doesn't improve because half of the time is spent making up from drunken fights. It's like casting Shia LaBeouf for your movie. You can do it, but if the role requires anything beyond jumping, falling and ducking, you're fucked.

I think social drinking is fun. Is it good for your relationship though? Well I'm at Rogues Gallery, drinking already today, so I might not be the best one to ask. You've got to look at your past relationships and see if alcohol was the cause of their downfalls.

See, in the beginning, when you're dating a guy and things are still shiny and new, lots of shit is excused. If you're a hot girl, guys will often let even more stuff slide by. You've got to be able see it on your own and be able to tell when he's getting fed up with your bullshit. What sometimes happens is that you start sleeping with him and everything seems great until that stuff you've been doing from day one (the stuff he now can't stand) sends him off into someone else's bed.

> "If that's how he feels, why wouldn't he just say that?"

For starters, most guys are complete pussies when it comes to being honest with a girl. Some guys feel they're really lucky to have any girl, much less a girl who would want to sleep with them and touch their penis. And if you're a pretty girl at that? Forget it! If you're way out of his league, you'll most likely never get the whole truth, except from me.

Here's how guys really feel about your drinking habits:

1. Drunken girls become jealous girls, and jealous girls become angry girls, who then become crying girls, who later become passed out girls. This cycle is about as much fun as getting a hand job on your honeymoon.

2. The "Houdini" is by far, the worst drunk girl move ever. Don't disappear while drunk!

3. Drunken sex is not hot; neither is you tasting like cigarettes and Jack Daniels every night.

4. *The 40-Year-Old Virgin* scene, in the car after the nightclub, is the best portrayal of a drunken girl of all time!

5. Don't pull a "Cast Away." People in shipwrecks forget what happened to them and how they got there, not people in bedrooms.

6. If you really aren't sure if "we" used a condom, and you'd like to know, don't ask us, instead look around the floor, guys flush condoms, not condom wrappers.

7. If you do go home with him, always brush your teeth in the morning! Put something useful in that big purse, toothbrushes are tiny!

8. Puking is a part of life. So is going to the gynecologist. Don't include your guy in either one of them.

9. Guys have heard the line, "Just so you know, I never do this kind of thing," even more times than you've lied about the number of people you've actually slept with. Yes, that many times!

10. Whoever it was that told you they don't mind taking care of you, or your wasted face friends at the end of the night, was a big fat liar!!

So play it safe and don't drink too much. How much is too much? Think of it like eating bad food. We all try to eat healthy.

Do we do it all the time?
No.
Do we wish that we did?
Yes.
Would we all be better off if we did?
Absolutely!

Of course we'll have those bender days now and again where things get a little bit out of hand. Just like eating junk food, it's fine to do once in a while. Drinking will happen, just try to keep the number of times that you become "that girl" to a low percentage, and you'll be just fine.

Five

Things You Should Never, Ever, Say...

People say some really crazy stuff to each other. Of course there are all different types of crazy. There's the Courtney Love koo koo and then the Gary Busey fucking insane! And somewhere in between those two are the rest of us. This is not about name calling or talking dirty, although we will be touching on those briefly, it's about uttering something that changes all the stakes, like say, I don't know, having someone tell you that they have "the herp" on your first date.

From the very moment that it's uttered, it won't be forgotten and nothing will ever be the same again.

Section One- The Lies

Guys are dumb, that's for sure (see I'm not always on their side ladies) and they'll often say some really dumb shit. Saying dumb shit to girls kind of falls in the same category as fighting with other boys in bars or grabbing a girl's breasts like they're made out of whatever it is that they put in those fun stress toys. Guys just do dumb shit. Why? Who knows.

> "The harder I grab, the hotter she'll get, and a little pinch to her nipples, chick's love that shit!"

Or, how about…

> -The guy who thinks that your pee hole is your clit!
> -The guy who asks you, "Did you come?" every ten seconds!
> -The guy who has a barbed wire tattoo around his arm!
> -The guy who tries to jam his fingers into you like he's sixteen!
> -The guy who calls you baby on your first date.
> -The guy who actually paid to see the last *The Fast and the Furious* movie two different times in the theater.
> -The guy who went along with him to see it.
> -The guy who wears his Bluetooth on a fucking date!

See, I could do an entire book just about lame guys, but I'd rather talk about girls.

My real problem with girls lying is a basic lack of creativity. See, girls will often tell the same exact lies to everybody that they date. So because of this mass-recycling effort, we've now heard the same ones used over and over again. Before you can even finish telling us the lie, we already know exactly how it's going to end. This causes three bad things to happen:

1. We're instantly reminded of every girl who has said the exact same thing before.

2. You no longer hold any credibility with us.

3. You've now been moved over to the "girls who say dumb shit" list. And you really don't want to be on this list, believe me.

So then, what are the lies that you should never, ever, say?

"Baby, I'm Pregnant... I Think."

Ask any guy, "Have you ever had a girl tell you that she was pregnant, just to see how you'd react to the question?"

From the now-classic "I think I'm pregnant" text message, to the foreboding announcement, "Um, I don't think that I should drink until I get my period."

This is the worst lie ever.

I can promise you that every guy is fully aware that unprotected sex tends to produce babies. And if she's Latino, or named Kate, you could end up with seven or eight of those little fuckers. We also know that while of course it "could" easily happen, no woman in her right mind should ever say that she is, in fact pregnant, if she's not one hundred percent sure that it's true. It drives guys absolutely crazy. It really should be completely off limits as a game or as a cute joke. I don't mess around with this stuff at all. As soon as a silly girl I'm dating gives me even the tiniest inkling that she's bad at taking her pill, I'll make her take it right in front of me while I'm standing there, and then I'll say to her,

> "Let me see under your tongue... lift it up...
> ok baby, now let's see the other side... good
> girlfriend... that's a good girlfriend... who's
> a good girlfriend? Who's a good girlfriend?
> Yes you are! Wanna go outside? Outside?
> You want to go in the car?"

> "Sometimes though, a girl might actually, really, legitimately, think that she is pregnant. What about then asshole?"

Look, whoever just had that thought out loud, you're a fucked up person. You're exactly the kind of girl I'm taking about. I hate girls like you. But I have an answer. You'll know if you're pregnant or not by taking a test! And then, when those little pink lines say that you are, you should go and take another test at your doctor's office. And if you still are, after all that, *then* you can say it!!!!

> "But tests are so expensive!" explains the
> dumb girl.

Yup they are. And so are babies! Have you ever watched that Jon and Kate show? That shit adds up fast! They really should have only kept six of those kids; eight's just way too many. But how do you pick, right? Simple. For starters, toss Aiden, the slow one with the glasses. Look, Asian or not, that kid will never master math. And Cara, the loud one who thinks that she's so cute, but is really just a snotty little stuck up bitch, she needs to go. Eleven or not, that little girl sucks! Those would be my votes anyway.

What a great idea! Jon should just have eight more kids with a different lady, and then have all the kids live together in a big house on a farm somewhere in Ohio and they do challenges each week. The winner from each week's show stays in the house, and the loser has to go live in foster care in Cleveland. Now there's your hit fucking TV show TLC! You're welcome!

All I'm saying is maybe it's just best to stop having sex all together if you can't even afford a pregnancy test. Condoms cost a whole lot less than diapers or Asian babies, trust me.

It's a pretty serious thing though, and yet girls will make it into a guessing game of sorts. I've heard stories where girls swore up and down that they were pregnant, and then came clean only a few hours later, finally admitting to their guy,

"I just wanted to see how you'd react."
Or
"I wanted you to call me back, you weren't answering your phone!"

Really? I mean *really*? Not cool ladies! I know that sometimes in life you really are late, and being late can happen for all kinds of reasons. I've been through it before. I think everyone has. It can be a very scary thing, that's for sure. It can also be a blessing, so if and when the time comes, and it's appropriate and actually true, be a woman about it and tell your guy with some class and maturity. Look, I'm not going to spend anymore time on this one, it would be like watching *Transformers* without Megan Fox in it… not really worth it to me. You either get this one, or you don't.

The Snow White Lies...

Snow White claimed to be as pure as snow, an innocent, sweet, fair young woman, but in all reality she was shacking up with seven dudes, and while I'm sure that Grumpy or Dopey may not have been getting any, at least a couple of those hobbits were hitting it. Then she went out and hooked up with some prince boy that she barely knew? What a little skank! Did anybody really buy her story? Well, not me!

These are the lies that you'll tell so that you don't feel like a complete slut. Just like Snow White living with seven dudes, sometimes girls get around more than they care to admit. I'm right there with you darling, why should you admit to it? The best thing you can do is to have no comment at all. Keep that stuff private. Saying nothing is always going to be better in the long run, than telling your guy Snow White lies. Here are my all time favorites...

"I'm not that kind of girl!"

-This usually is said about an hour before we have sex.

-Wait it's opposite day, right?

-But you banged my friend last weekend?

-So, blow job good, swallow bad. OK, got it...

-That's what every girl says who IS that kind of girl!

"I just want you to know, I never do this."

-Which part? My dick in your mouth, or my dick in your mouth after we just had sex?

-Honey, it doesn't work if you say it right after we finish!

-Says the girl already in my elevator!

-Wait, the last nine hours we had? Or just this morning?
-What, forget to put on panties? No worries, happens to me all the time.

"This is so not like me!"

-That was an amazing blow job, you really are having beginner's luck!
-So I'm the "one" then? Yes, I KNEW IT!
-Me either, I'm so glad that we're both on the same page.

"I only sleep with guys who are my boyfriends."

-How long does that take? Can I be him for tonight?
-Says the half naked girl who's already holding my dick in her hand.
-Can we just cuddle then?
-But you already have a boyfriend...

"I never get that drunk!"

-This week? Or just on Mondays?
-Your Facebook is spreading lies then.
-10 shots will do that to a girl.
-And claim it?

If you're wondering why guys say these kinds of things, you can blame the girls who've come before you. Guys have heard these lines so many times before that even at the small chance that you're really being honest about it, you've already reminded us of the last girl who said that exact same thing as you. It's the same as when a guy comes up to you and says,

-"So you come here often?"
-"Do you believe in love at first sight?"
-"How much does a polar bear weigh? Enough to break the ice, hi I'm D..."

Guys have their pick up lines and girls have their Snow White lies. Both sides are completely full of shit. So limit your use of these old standards and once you do, you may find that things go more smoothly for you and your date will probably take you more seriously. Just like with a governor, athlete or pop star it's very easy to see through all the nonsense. So be careful, because once credibility is lost, it stays lost and will haunt you forever. And even if you end up being together, he will always remember how in the very beginning, you swore up and down that you wouldn't, but then you did. He will also wonder what else you've lied about. And besides, saying those types of things doesn't really work anyway. It doesn't change anything, you don't look more innocent, and you still seem "easy." It's just like saying...

"With all due respect..."

It's meant to show respect and make it crystal clear that before the next statement, whatever it may be, no disrespect should be taken. But it only works if it's followed by something that doesn't offend anyone.

You can't say, "With all due respect, I think you're a complete dumb ass!" And you also can't say, "I never do this!" And then go ahead and fucking do it anyway!

I've had a girl actually say to me, "I never do this!" while I was still inside her!

Section Two- The Exaggerations

Girls, girls, girls, you crack me up! Listen, with all due respect, you some silly bitches! The exaggerations are my absolute favorites. Just like the Snow Whites lies, we know that you're completely full of shit, but these are more hilarious. Whether they're being told just to be nice or told to impress, one thing is guaranteed: we ain't buying it. First up...

"I'm a model"

Okay, listen up ladies.

> If you talk me into buying shots from your tray at a bar, you're not a model.

> If you have to pay someone else to take photos of you, you're not a model.

> If you wear a tank top with a brand on it during your "modeling," you're not a fucking model.

> If you have to put on your own makeup when you "model," you're not a model.

There are pretty girls everywhere, and some of them are promo girls who do get paid for representing brands. This does not make them models. Lots of girls have had photographers take pictures of them. They pay for these photos and even have a pretty little book to show off to their friends. This does not make you a model. If you don't have an agent, or a daily rate, or an eating disorder, you are most likely *not* a real model.

I've only known three models in my day, and they did shoots for magazines, billboards, and print ads. Real models charge a lot and don't have to wear Jack Daniels tank tops. They have a daily rate, not an hourly wage, and they fly to work. They also don't have kids to check in on. If I hear one more shot girl tell me she needs to "check in" with her sitter, to see if she can stay after her shift is done, (models don't have shifts by the way) I swear, I'm going to write a parenting book! You are, however, the prettiest shot girl that I've seen here this whole week. So good job on that one. Next up...

"OMG, It's so big!!"

I love this one! Guys have a general idea if what they have to work with is enough, but that doesn't answer the bigger question: what have you had to work with? While we'd all like to believe that what we have is enough, we're never really positive. I mean who wouldn't want another inch or two, right? So it's always great to hear the girl say...

"OMG it's so big!"

And it would be even more believable if you were the only person that I'd ever slept with, but sadly, you're not my first, and every girl I've been with tells me that it's big. Some even call it the monster! Sounds great, right? I must be huge? I'm not though. I'm average. Most guys are just average. I've peeked in the locker room, and I've been on the web. Believe me, I know without a doubt that I'm not huge. So I wonder, what's really going on here? I do appreciate the support. It's always nice to hear, but you need to know that most guys won't believe you, ok? So moving on...

"I've never felt like this before, I know you're the one!"

Says the girl who, two weeks from now, will cheat on me at her friend's birthday party.

"I have never felt like this before!"

What does that even mean?

"The One?" You mean like Neo? Like I'm going to save you and Trinity, and if we have any time left over, we can go grab Morpheus, too? What happens if I don't agree with you that I'm the one? It's like the whole soul mate deal. Do I even get a vote? I can't be your soul mate if we meet at a bar, make out, and have one great night of sex. I can't be. It doesn't work like that. For me it doesn't anyway. I also can't be the one if I say to you that I'm not the one! We both have to be on the same page for it to be a real thing, and that's if it even exists at all. If it does, then I think maybe it's like unicorns; of course we all know that they exist, but we just can't see them!

You should be seeing a pattern here. It's all about you being sincere, it's about the fact that every girl says to us, "You're the one." That's why guys never take it seriously. Every girl says, "I have never felt like this before." We've heard it so much that it means nothing now. If you say it after a year and a half of dating, we may bite, but after only three months, you're coming off a little Courtney Love. Whenever a girl tells me these sorts of things, I have to get all Keyser Söze on her and explain that our relationship never really existed. Guys will pull back when you start to exaggerate about love, life and penis size. I don't have to be "the biggest" that you've ever seen, or "the best" that you've ever had. If you're dating a guy who needs to hear those things all the time, I'd say he's way too insecure to support you or a family. Trust me, he will not make a good husband. Ditch him now. You'll thank me later.

Section Three- The "There's Only One Right Answer" Questions

Loaded questions. This one could get messy. It looks just like a normal question, only it comes with drama, apologies and no sex for at least one week. This is easily one of the most frustrating parts about dating a girl. Guys know that being completely honest should always be our goal. We aim to be one hundred percent honest and up front with you about everything, but that's all before Beth starts in with her, "But what if" questions. Or Ashlee hits us with her, "Let's say that you had to pick one" dilemmas.

These questions seem to come crashing down out of thin air. It usually starts out as a cute game:

"If I was burned in a fire would you still want to be with me?"

Or

"If I lost both of my legs in a bad car wreck and then had to be in a wheel chair, would you still date me?"

Textbook loaded questions, right? So what is it exactly that you'd like him to say?

You'd like to hear:

"Baby of course I would still be with you, don't be silly!"

I'd say the real answers though, go something more like this…

"Honey, I wouldn't be dating you if you had a cracked toe nail!"

"Do you mean like Travis Barker burned up? Or like that lady that was on the Oprah show, how burned up are we talking here?"

"Yes, I would wheel you around as long as we got handicap parking."

"I think you'd be much happier if we found you a nice boy to roll around with. You two could be chair buddies!"

See, guys want to tell you the truth, but they'll lie as soon as they realize that the truth is going to cause some major drama...

-Scene: Sitting on couch, Seinfeld goes to commercial-

You: Which one of my friends would you want to have sex with if you never met me?

Me: Honey, I don't think about your friends like that.

You: Come on don't be a pussy, I'm not going to tell them. I don't really care I promise, I just want to know.

Me: I'm not attracted to your friends, I couldn't even say...

You: But let's just say, like if you had to pick one.

Me: I think this is a bad idea. Why would I have to pick one?

You: You're being so lame, just pick one!

Me: I don't know, I guess maybe Jen, she seems fun... Yeah, Jen would be my pick.

You: You would fuck Jen!? You're disgusting. Why, because of her huge fake tits? Is that how you want me to look? Because I can get them if that's what turns you on, asshole....

-End Scene-

-Continued... Three weeks later while watching trashy reality TV-

Me: God, that girl's implants are awful, why do girls do that to themselves?

You: Awful? What about Jen? I thought that was your thing. You know, I still can't believe you fucking said that...

-Argument ensues-

This game suuuuuuucks! Why do we have to play it? Or any variation of, "Who's my hottest friend?" Or "Which of my friends has the best body?" These games are awful! There are no safe answers, and really no way to give a real answer. Trust me, every guy knows, without question, *exactly* which one of your friends he would like to fuck. He knows the answer without even having to think about it, and most likely, you already know his answer too. He will never tell you her name, so don't even bother asking him. Besides all you'd get is his second round draft pick (sports talk for not the one he really wants). It shouldn't really matter to you who he says anyway. It's not worth getting upset over. Believe me, it's not like he would ever try to do it, or if you two were to break up, he would go right for her. Most guys aren't that cruel. But let's just say for the sake of argument that he did go for her, and they hooked up, what does that say about your choice in girlfriends? Trust me, it's best for you to just…

"Let it be" – Paul McCartney

Now, here are some other really terrible questions, be aware that you're wasting your time even asking them. Nothing good will come from the real answers, and I promise you, most likely, your guy is not dumb enough to ever tell you the truth!

What are we?
Sorry, but we would rather get Q-tips inserted in the head of our penis than answer this one. By the way, fun fact: if your guy has had this done to him before, it means he was tested for Gonorrhea!

What are you thinking right now?
Only appropriate if we're on a sinking ship or in a hospital.

Did you go inside me?
Really? Are we going to un-have sex now? Why even ask after?

How many girls have you been with?
☺ *You look pretty today!*

How much do you love me?
Um, more than your father, can we have sex now?

Do I look fat?
If I answer this will I ever get a blowjob again?

You agree with me, right? She's trying to ruin my life?
Um, yes honey, the coffee shop girl does mess up your order a lot!

Joe Montana Football on Sega Genesis is NOT the best video game ever!
You shut your fucking mouth!

Do you think she is prettier than me?
Only if you're into obvious beauty, which I'm not.

What would you do if I died?
I would miss you...a lot?

Do you really love me?
Yes, I really like you... wait what?

You're the best I've ever had, am I the best you've ever had?
Yes, of course, you are the only girl I even remember having sex with.

My point is this, have you ever had the guy who asked you two seconds after sex, "Did you get off?" Or while in the middle of going down on you, he stops to ask if you're about to get off? How much does that suck? See it's just like that. Who says boys and girls are so different?

Section Four- The Stuff You Say to Him and Don't Really Mean

This last part is the stuff that comes out in anger. It comes out fast and loud and it can't be taken back. The good part is, it means that you really have passion for him. Think about it... you never seem to have these problems at work, or with people you see only once in a while. Nope, it's always with the ones you love; they can make you fucking crazy like no other. Fighting with the one you love has some simple ground rules though. Say things that will make you feel better, and then be prepared to say sorry for about two hours. Well, if only it were that simple. I won't try to be clever here, I'm just going to lay it out for you, some of these things are as close to unforgivable as you can possibly get. Never, ever, say them...

-"I hate you."
-"At least he could get me off."
-"I'm going to go out and fuck (insert name here) tonight!"
-"Don't ever call me again."
-"I never really loved you."
-"I faked it."
-"Well I slept with (insert name here)!"
-"I'm only with you because it's safe."
-"Do you know how many guys want to fuck me?"
-"You have a small dick!" (For real... never, ever, say this one.)
-"Your own mother doesn't love you."
-"Even your friends don't like you."
-"Your friends like me better, they tell me all the time, I should just leave you!" (Don't quote people because we will ask them.)

-"I can't believe I'm even with you."
-"My friends think you're a loser!"
-"I hate your family!"
-"I never should have broken up with my ex!"
-"I wish I never met you!"
-"I don't even know why you moved here."
-"I wish you would move back home!"
-"You are such a pussy!"
-"I wish you were dead!"
-"I'm fucking Matt Damon!"(Wait, Really?)
-"Don't you think that by (insert age here) you should have your shit together?"
-"I'm going to leave you any day now!"
-"You're lucky I don't cheat on you. Do you know how easy that would be for me to do?"

I know what you're thinking. "Come on, there's no way girls actually say those things!" The funny thing about this chapter is that every time I've ever had a girlfriend, and told her that I think one of her friends is a complete hot mess, she'd always tell me, "Be quiet, I love my friends!"

Tara?
"I love her. I do. I love Tara, but she's a slut."

Kayla?
"Kayla is my girl, but she is a little skanky. So what?"

And Lisa?
"Well, Lisa is a hot fucking mess."

And Sarah's not?
"Sarah's a dirty bitch. That's my girl though"

So don't pretend that you "don't know any girls like this."

Because you DO know girls like this! Look around at your friends!

Six

Put the Phone Down!

I want to start by telling you a little bit about my own phone. I'm a Blackberry guy for life. The iPhone never made much sense to me. I mean, why would I want to watch a movie on my phone when I have a fucking TV that works just fine? And angry birds, is for the birds if you ask me, that game gave me my first grey hair! Anyhow, I have an unlimited plan now, and it means that I have all the minutes and texts in the whole wide world to use as I see fit. I waited a long time for this. You see, I use to have a plan called the 5000-minute talk whenever the fuck you wanted to plan. Guess what else? It still wasn't enough! I went over my minutes all the time! I'd have to call into the customer service agents and state my case.

"What do you do for work sir? We see that you already have our best nation-wide calling plan, but even with that you seem to be making an awful lot of phone calls. Sir by the way, this call is being recorded for quality assurance, and if you'd like, you can participate in our customer serv…"

"NOOOO! Thank you, but no, listen I went over my minutes again, how much is that shit going to cost me this time?"

$469.17. What a mess! It figures though. I have over a thousand contacts in my phone. Eighteen of those are from other countries. I have two cell batteries which I carry around with me, and last year I finally threw in the towel and started doing email from the phone. Yep, I'll be one of the first ones to get that cell phone cancer that they always talk about. And would you like to know why? Because I fucking hate Bluetooths!

"Hey, you know how I know you're gay?"
"You have a fucking Bluetooth!"

More than all that though, I love sending those text messages. I think that they're wonderful and I'm full on the new fangled texting bandwagon. I use thousands of them a month, maybe more. So I tell you all that, to tell you this,

I absolutely fucking hate cell phones!

Seriously, I really do hate them. Sure, they're easily one of the greatest, if not *the* greatest invention of our lifetime. I get all that, but I also remember a beautiful time long before them.

We used to have these little things called mobile pagers. I got my first one when I was in middle school. I was like Doogie Howser, M.D. only without the ability to prescribe Vicodin. Then I got an even better one in high school. I had a black Motorola to start with, and later moved on to a fancy blue one. It had a slide-in case with an awesome clip for my belt. I was dope! The miggity, miggity, miggity, miggity Mac Daddy. Did I really need a pager? No, of course not. Though at the time, it seemed like it was a very useful thing for me. It served a purpose, I suppose.

There were all these special codes for things, little secret meanings between you and the girl you were dating. We had re-invented the whole purpose for even having a pager. Its original job was to tell you to run to the nearest phone and call the phone number back because super important news was waiting for you.

Well, we were 12, 13, 14 and so on, so what important news did we have waiting for us that we needed a pager? Absolutely none. Instead, we used them to send texts in our own little language. It was great to get a late night page before bedtime, 222222 meant, "I love you!" We had decided on that one together (my girlfriend and I). It was our own secret code, which no one else knew about it. We were like prison inmates, and her dad was the warden. There was also the "69" beep. That was the best one, though at thirteen we didn't really have a fucking clue how that all worked, but the warden sure did, and so there went her pager.

So around this time, the only people I knew who had cell phones were all adults. My dad had what they called the "bag phone." I don't ever recall seeing him use it, not even once. It was for the car, and only to be used if I were "bleeding" as he so sternly put it. So when his work gave him a flip phone, I was super hopeful that the "bleeding rule" had changed. But it didn't. We had a flip phone before anybody else I knew. In fact, we didn't even have call waiting on our house phone yet! Sadly though, I was told again that it was for extreme emergencies only, or really important business calls. I guess they were very expensive to operate, and we weren't rich by any means.

Let me get you out of the '90s and into the year 2000!

-Singing in falsetto-

"In the year 2000… In the year 2000…"

Erin Brockovich is slutting it up, Leo is telling Rose that she's stupid for coming back for him, and little Elián is floating around Miami somewhere on a box, or was it an inner tube? Let's not forget RU-486 gets full US approval. Big year indeed! See, once pagers died out, cell phones became more of a commonplace thing. Of course they still were considered very much of a luxury. People had them, but most had maybe only two hundred minutes per month to use, and again, that was only for very special occasions. They still weren't for daily chatting.

Well, that all changed very quickly. I soon had the Nokia 6110. Look it up, it was a great phone, and I'm pretty sure that I still hold the all-time high score for snake. It was given to me for work and it was awesome. I remember thinking to myself the day I got it…

"Who the fuck do I have to call? What am I going to do with this thing?"

I didn't really understand the whole concept behind it. Why would I even need to have this thing? To stay connected? Okay, but about what? Work had given it to me, and they covered the bill, so I took it. I won't bore you with much more of this stuff, the point is this: we all eventually got cell phones and once we did, we never looked back again.

So what does all this have to do with dating, you may ask? Everything!

The cell phone has changed dating more than any other invention, even more than the birth control pill. It has become a nasty thorn in all of our dating lives. A new drug of choice, and we're all becoming addicted to it. It's fast, cheap and easy to get. We try to tell ourselves that it helps us stay closer to one another and keeps us more connected to people, but the opposite is now happening.

OMG, TTYL, ☺, Lmao, ...

Girls love their cell phones. The only thing that they might love even more is their digital camera. Now that they're one in the same, we have a big problem.

Cell phones can cause so many problems for relationships.

But before we dive balls deep into this one, I'd just like to add something. This whole phone thing is happening just about everywhere you look. It goes for the guys as well. Look, if you have little brothers or sisters, you need to step in and set some serious ground rules for them. You become the parent, if that's what it takes! You know that they really shouldn't have their own cell phones (especially at such a young age), but fine, these days most of them do, and I get that. But if they're going to have one, trust me, they don't need to have picture messaging with it. Get that shit off their phones fast! Look, if we can't even count on *High School Musical* actresses to keep their clothes on, what makes you really think that your "Miley" wannabe sister isn't standing in a bathroom right now posing in front of the mirror, arm stretched out, making pouty lips, with her leg up on the sink?

"Not my little sister, she knows better than that!"

Well, don't you sound just like the mother completely in shock on the six o'clock evening news...

"We've never had any problems with her before, she's a really good girl, and she always gets good grades. We don't even let her talk to boys, I don't understand how this could have happened!"

I'm not going to ramble on about this one, but please realize it's very important. If parents really knew exactly what was going on with their own children, there would be no drug overdosing, no teen pregnancy and no drunk driving. But that stuff all still happens. See, parents are designed by nature to have no fucking clue. So it's up to you. Please protect your sisters, brothers, nieces and nephews!

There, I've said my piece.

Section One- Phone Manners...

So you have a phone, he has a phone, everyone has a phone. When you first start dating somebody new, you have to ease in slowly to get used to one another's good and bad phone habits. If you're a person who can't be away from your phone for even an hour, then it may be hard for you to understand why he'd want to eat dinner and do so without you texting the entire meal. It's all about showing respect to your date. You need to show respect. Some men won't admit to this, but I'll tell you anyway,

    While sex is great, respect is really the key ingredient to keeping a man happy.

    You need to make him feel like a man, and you know you wouldn't be texting at dinner in front of a man whom you had true respect for. He knows this, you know this, the waiter knows this, and even the pretty boy staring at you from the next table over knows this. Men need respect to function, almost like we need air. It's so important for you to lead by example. You both need to be focused in on one another. Otherwise, what's the point? Why even bother to show up? Between receiving emails from department stores, Facebook updates and your wing girl's new dating crisis of the moment, your phone has a lot of shit to talk to you about. All of it can wait. Trust me, life will go on, even if you can't see at that very moment that...

    "All Women's Jeans are 20% off, now through the 20th only at Express!"

    You will survive this, I promise you. Believe it or not, it is possible to ignore your cell phone for small increments of time.

You can't use them in hospitals or on airplanes (even if you're Alec Baldwin) and, unless you're a complete asshole, at the movies. So why would you think that on a date is a good time to do this? People seem to know better than to answer a text message while in a work meeting, especially in front of their boss, but how come they can't keep from doing it during their date? Which is more important, love or work?

Plain and simple, it's a huge turn off for your date and extremely disrespectful. Your date wouldn't bring along his buddy to dinner with him, how would you feel if he did? Well then, you shouldn't bring along any of your friends either, even if they're only there by way of a four-inch screen.

The only time it would maybe be appropriate to check your phone during a meal is if you were Oprah or Martha Stewart. Those bitches have important shit going on! Employees, lawsuits, businesses, and franchises to run. You do not. Oprah is so fucking huge that Microsoft Word just auto corrected her name for me as I was typing and misspelling it. Does that happen when I misspell your name? Nope. So just be glad that you have the luxury of being able to enjoy a nice meal without having to check your phone every five seconds, because those ladies do not.

"But what if it's a real emergency?"

Like what? An earthquake in Wisconsin? A fifty-year storm in Kentucky? What possible emergency will you make all better by answering a phone call? Maybe if you were, say, a doctor? That I could understand. Even if you were a doctor, don't they have other doctors? This is not the small town of Grady, Georgia, and you're not Doc Hollywood! Someone else will handle it until you finish your plate of pasta.

People like to think of themselves as the last action hero; whatever Jack Slater, you're not the only person who's capable of saving the day. It's really gotten out of hand these days, and it's damaging to all types of relationships. The fact that people can even utter out loud, "Well, what if there is a real emergency?" is a purely narcissistic thought! Do you really, honestly believe that you're going to be able to do something about the "crisis" that's already taken place?

Sometimes, (maybe one time in a million) you're the only person who can actually help out. Like little Frodo Baggins[*], he was the only one! I had a girlfriend once who thought that she was Frodo, always asking me about some ring? "I need a ring! Where is the ring?" WTF, I had to get out of there, and fast! Don't be a girl who pulls a Frodo! Guys don't like it. The bottom line is this: keep the phone in your purse, or better yet, leave it in the car.

---

[*] Authors note: For all you die hard Lord of the Rings people out there, I'm fully well aware that Gollum, or "Sméagol" as he was also often called, was a member of the secluded branch of early Stoorish Hobbits, and that his real name, in "Westron" was actually "Trahald." So don't try me, ok! I know that it was he, who was really the ring obsessed Hobbit, and not Frodo, but I didn't like the joke the other way around. So please fuck off. I don't need you to send me emails about this. God, you're acting just like Sam right now, quit being a little bitch.

Section Two- Phone Sluts

As you all probably know, sexting has become a normal part of today's dating world, and, honestly, after as many stories as we've seen in our mainstream press involving just about every age, type of person, and profession that there is, I think it's safe to say that just about everybody's sent or received a sext.

Obviously there's a huge double standard here. Guys love the photos, but as soon as girls send them, they become damaged goods.

Here's the thing. Girls already know that it's a bad idea, which is why when they send them, they cover up their faces. If you don't trust him enough to have your face in the photo, why would you ever send him one to begin with?

I wish I could tell you that I've never asked a girl to send me naked photos, but I'd be lying to you, because of course I have. Do I show them to other people? Yes, I do. However, I would never show a picture of any girl I'm actually dating, to anybody. That's just how I operate though, you may not be so lucky with whomever you're sending yours to. You may be wondering who else would be sending me naked photos. That's a great question.

Girls have sent me naked photos of themselves for all kinds of different reasons. Sure, some were my actual girlfriends at the time, but the others were usually one-night stands, or girls that I'd hooked up with once, maybe twice. They'd send these photos at random times, on random days, almost like a greeting card: "Hey just wanted to say hi, miss you!"

There were several girls who, years after we'd hooked up, even after some had *married*, still sent me photos. Yes, you read that right. They were married and still continued to send me naked pictures. I remember being out with a buddy and he called "bullshit" on me when I told him that this happens. I told him, "There are at least six girls in my phone right now I could text and ask for a naked photo, and I bet I get at least four pictures back before we even pay the bill."

"No way, that's bullshit!" he said. So I sent the same text out to all six of them, "Hey, just thinking about you, wish I had a photo, I forget how hot your body is!"

Guess what? I had three photos within ten minutes. One of the girls was an ex of mine who had recently gotten married, and the other two were girls I'd hooked up with.

So, either they were all single (which is pretty fucking doubtful) and ran to the nearest bathroom mirror just to snap a quick photo for me, or the photos were old and already in their phones. You tell me. I can't explain that one. It's beyond the realm of logic.

I'll tell you what I do know though, it's happening everywhere, all over the country. And by the way, I was five for six by the time we paid our bill. And yes, I showed the entire table. After all, I had to prove my point!

Poker Face...

So my last job was basically executing huge live events for corporate clients. Concerts, festivals, sporting events, and so on. Due to the large scale of these events, we'd have to hire temp staff to help us out. We'd hire them from "modeling agencies," and they were always pretty girls, usually between the ages of eighteen and twenty-five. We would be in a different city every week, all over the country. I'd have between fifteen to twenty new girls to look after. If they were messing around with their phones, texting or what not, I'd say to them:

Me: Cool phone, can I see it?

Temp Girl: Sure.

Now, this became the pivotal moment because right after the "sure" came a huge fucking clue. It always seemed to go the same way. They'd hand me the phone and say nothing, until I started pushing buttons, and then I'd hear in a pure panic, "Wait, don't look at my pictures please!"

Jackpot!

Sometimes as they handed me their phone I'd just plain out ask them, "Hey got any cool pictures in here?"

There was pure terror in the eyes of the guilty each and every time. Sometimes I wouldn't have the phone for more than a second because as soon as I asked the question, they'd grab it right back out of my hands. The good girls though, would let me play with their phones without a care in the world.

Then things got a little crazy. Fucked up is a better choice of words. A guy that I was working with during this time (whose name I don't remember) had somehow caught on to the fact that I was always asking to see the girls' phones. Joe, we'll call him, asked me why I did it, and I explained to him my theory: that every girl had naked photos and it was funny to ask to look at their phones because that's when they'd give away the answer.

"Wait, so do they? Do you ever see them? Do they ever show them to you?" He asked, suddenly now very excited about all this.

"Well yeah, sometimes they do," I said calmly. "Other times they'll hold it out for me to see, but if I ask them what kind of pictures they have, they'll say, 'Just me in a bikini.' Then I'll tell them, 'Oh, I thought it was going to be something good,' and that's when they'll usually admit to it, but they always say something about the pictures being only for their boyfriend's eyes."

"So then how do you get to see them?" he persisted.

"Well, once they admit to it, and they see that I don't really give a shit and that I don't think they're slutty for having them in the first place, I'm usually allowed to see them, and sometimes they'll even send them right to my phone. But first they'll make me promise up and down that I won't show anybody else. It's usually a tit, ass or vagina shot, and rarely will their faces be in them. I'm guessing that's maybe why they don't mind if I see them?"

"I can't believe this, that's amazing!" He said in disbelief. "Does this happen every weekend?"

I smiled.

Well I really should have paid closer attention to his level of interest. I figured he was just excited. Little did I know, right at that very moment a dirty, creepy monster was being born. I had made the conditions perfect for its immaculate conception. Shit, what had I done? He was, and actually is, a really a good guy. I feel like I need to stress that before I continue.

Soon after I'd admitted to the motivation behind my little game of poker face with these girls, Joe came up with a new work rule. He decided that the girls could no longer have their cell phones out during the event.

"There's way too much texting going on. They're getting paid over twenty dollars an hour," he explained. "There's no need for them to be on their phones during our event. So, from now on I want the girls to leave their phones in their purses. We'll lock them in our stock room, and they can get them back on their breaks."

How in the world I didn't see this at the time still amazes me. Do you see it yet? Well, get there faster! He had our entire staff's cell phones locked up in one room. A room that only we had the key to.

I KNOW!!!

I guess maybe it's not really as bad as it sounds?

Who am I trying to kid? It was Super Bad! I swear though, I didn't have the slightest clue what was going on… at first.

Was I shocked? No, not really, but I was a bit wigged out. I remember it like it was four years ago. Which is when it happened. I went into the stock room during our event, and Joe was already inside, smiling ear to ear.

Joe: Lock the door dude.

Me: What's up man?

Joe: Ok, I already know what you're going to say, but fuck you because this is awesome, check this out!

I already knew what was about to happen as he started to lift up his hand. He held up a phone to show me, and on the small screen, there she was, a hot, naked girl holding up her phone to a mirror, with a nearly perfect body in the frame. I instantly recognized her face.

Kayla! That was her name (but not really, wink wink). She was one of our staff for the weekend, and in fact, she was standing about ten feet away, working on the other side of the door. I stared a bit longer - at this point why the fuck not? She looked amazing. I mean really, really good. Maybe that was all in my head though. The whole thing was very surreal, like having a secret super hero power. X-ray vision came to mind. I mean, here was this smoking hot girl, a girl that we'd met only a day earlier, standing there completely naked. It was wild. Really, how could you not look? Well you wouldn't have, would you? Go ahead Christian, I guess you're up again.

"Oh, good for you!"

Me: Joe, what, I mean, how did you...

Joe: I just decided to look man, and you know what? You were so right. Every phone except for one had naked photos!

Me: Dude, you looked at all of them? This is so not ok.

Joe: Do you want see the best one?

Me: No, Joe I don't, ok, look this is so wrong!

See, that's what I probably should have said. I mean, that's really the only reasonable response that I could have had, but look, I promised you before that this book would be completely honest, so I'll continue on with the story for your sake, but I just think you should know, that on a scale of one to ten, for how bad I feel about this now, a ten being the highest, I'm at about a three. But it's a big three, like a three with a huge fucking exclamation point. Feel better? Me neither.

Here's what really happened…

Me: Yeah, I want to fucking see it! Is it Teri? Tell me that it's Teri please? This is crazy Joe, how long have you been doing this shit? Wait, is Sarah naked too? Or Kelly? Please say that Kelly is!

Joe: I told you bro, all but one of them. There are all kinds of photos too, lots of boobs, a few asses and lots of dicks actually. These girls are fucking wild. There are even some action shots!

Me: What the fuck man!

Joe: I know! You totally called it!

We were like scientists who'd discovered a whole new species of girl:

> **Whore-a-la-tis**: *Believed to be direct descendants of the scallywag family, not thought to be a monogamous species, often mating with several different partners, including their own sex on spring break trips. Emotionally unstable and self-destructive, little else is known about their daily routines. In the wild they prefer to feed on grilled chicken salads and have an orange skin tone during the winter months. Real hair color unknown.*

What was occurring was a true breakthrough in our completely unprofessional field study. With phone after phone, Joe provided me with concrete substantial evidence. I observed and made notes, for science of course, and was completely at a loss for words. I knew it was fucked up, but how could I not look? To even suggest that would have been ridiculous. So for the next ten minutes, in that little stock room, we became pioneers of a new sexual study. For the betterment of mankind, we forged ahead and performed the creepy, and most likely illegal task that we'd found ourselves called upon to execute. For some reason, at the time, it really didn't feel that wrong to me. It seemed somehow better than looking into a window where the shade was left up, and way less intrusive than a secret peephole.

I mean let's think about this, we've all walked past a window naked before, not necessarily hoping to be observed, and if you've ever stayed in a hotel, say in Nashville or Milwaukee, well chances are, the peephole wasn't listed as part of the hotel's lovely amenities. With this stuff though? It was like the photos were taken with intent to distribute. Like I said, most of the girls made sure their faces were out of the shot. Why I wonder? It seemed to imply that the expectations were clear that someone would be enjoying the view, besides the intended recipient. Here is what I remember - vividly, I might add...

> -The girl who told us about her little sister that she was so worried about and wanted to keep boys away from- Topless!

> -The girl who told us that she was going to school to become a kindergarten teacher- Fully nude!

> -The girl with the pretty Jesus cross around her neck- Kitty shot!

> -The girl who talked all about not being anything like "those kind of girls"- Topless!

> -The girl who was so quiet with almost no personality- Topless!

> -The girl that made sure to tell us that all guys suck and are sex obsessed- Bent over vagina shot! Classic! Go big or go home!

Now of course I know that these photos were supposed to be private. So maybe it was wrong to be judging them. I still can't believe it though; did girls really believe that only the person they sent it to would be the person seeing it? Since when did guys suddenly become so trustworthy? All I've ever heard was that guys are dogs, guys cheat, guys are shady, and so on.

Girls were always being very vocal about their skepticism of guys and their ability to be trusted completely. So why would a girl ever think that sending a photo of herself naked to her boyfriend, not a husband mind you, but just a boyfriend, was a smart idea? Maybe it was like when a guy sends flowers to his girlfriend's work instead of just sending them to her house.

Wait, there's a reason for that? Sorry guys...

We only do that because we know that everyone at the office (girls, that is, office guys will usually just talk shit) will gush over them with you. You'll feel special and your work wing girls will tell you over and over again how pretty your flowers are, which in turn will make them seem even more beautiful in your eyes. So maybe that's it? Girls must know that if our bros see the naked photo and rave to us about how hot it is, then we'll think that you're even sexier than we did before? Hmmm, I think I may be on to something here. Do they give out awards for breaking this sort of stuff down? No? Well maybe they should!

Anyway, our experiment was super short lived. Guilt, mixed with the fact that we never had any Asians (Joe's favorite) working for us, got him to lose interest fairly quickly. So although you and I both know that this thing they now call "sexting" is out of control, at least we know from this particular field study that it's been a problem way longer than anyone cares to admit.

Those same girls are most likely mothers now who will soon be giving their own little ones cell phones, probably by age seven because they got theirs by age twelve, vicious cycle indeed! Well, score one for the young boys of today I guess. When I was little all we had was ten-year-old *Playboys*, and let me tell you, the girls from the seventies didn't exactly do much for my inexperienced mind. At least the boys who'll be looking at your daughters will be around their same age, right?

Section Three- Phone Rules

Will somebody please submit this next section to the U.S. Congress because I believe that it needs to be made into law. I think that instead of calling this section "Phone Rules," we should have called it, "Daryl releases his inner Jewish lady." 'Cause I'm about to spout off the phone rules that I think everybody should live by, and it may take a while. Oy veh, watch out, here comes the Yenta. Speaking of Jews, why didn't they ask Mel Gibson to play the Jew hunter in *Inglourious Basterds*? That could have been a huge career turn around for him! Poor old Mel, he needs some Danny Glover back in his life!

Ok, so here are my rules in no particular order:

1. Ringtones...

Listen, nobody cares what band you like or what song you feel really defines you as a person. Tell me what's wrong with a plain old simple ring? Do you really love Fergie so much that you want to hear her voice ten times an hour? Should "Smack That" really define anyone as a person?

"My phone's about to ring! Somebody cue Lady Gaga... oh sorry, yeah, she can't make it right now, she's out shopping for masks. Alright fine then, how about some Katy Perry?"

Of course, I understand that the argument could be made that it's much easier to tell if your phone's the one that's ringing, and not somebody else's. The only problem with doing this is it requires you to keep your phone set to full blast at all times. Well, I thank you for that. And really, everyone should thank you. I'm with you. I mean who does-n't need a little dose of Taylor Swift early in the morning?

Maybe you have a few songs assigned for those spe-cial friends of yours and you're worried about how you'd be able to tell who's calling you without them? Well, how about you just look down at your phone when you hear it ring? Matter of fact, you could use that vibrate feature combined with the awesome power of sight! Amazing right? It really does work. Plus, that way, I wouldn't have to hear Rihanna screaming "What's my name?" while I'm trying to order my fucking coffee.

See, everyone wins.

2. Ringback tones...

No matter what you think, I promise you they're not awe-some. I'm sure that Rihanna loves them though.

3. Texting while someone is standing there talking to you...

This is a huge turn off. It shows that you're incapable of un-plugging yourself from your own daily bullshit. If it's gotten to the point that the people on the other end of your "LOLs" and "OMGs" are more important to you than the ones stand-ing right there in front of you, well, congratulations... you pretty much suck. Go play in traffic.

4. Texting at the movies...

Fuck you. I mean seriously fuck you! I would love to stab you in the jaw.

5. Texting in the car while you're driving...

Um, look, here's the thing about that. I know you're probably very careful while you're doing it, but I still think it's a risky thing to do. I like you, and it would really suck if something bad happened to you! As a matter of fact, I would just like to tell you right now that you look really pretty today, and thank you for buying my book and supporting me, and...

Wait, what? You STOLE this book!? Okay forget everything I just said. I have a fun little game for you to try. Have a few drinks and then see how well you can text the following sentence while driving:

"Uo, Hobcbq edfoug, whdhqdfqb dbqdk qdnljdw dlllnd, jbljl nlnlkl nlknlk, qoub fo u bdou qwd!"

If you make less than two errors, call me and I'll give you a dollar. Remember though, you must be going at least forty-five miles an hour.[*]

---

[*] Don't actually try this game unless you are a trained professional. Or do, but promise not to sue us subsequent to your attempt.

6. Calling with absolutely nothing to say...

So you just called him again, even though you spoke to him two hours earlier, and one hour before that. I know that you really miss him, and that you just had to tell him that there was nothing in the mail for him today! The thing is, sometimes we have nothing to say. "We" as in you and me. Both of us.

We're at work, working, and you're doing whatever it is you do all day. The phone rings, I answer, and you ask me for the fourth time that afternoon...

-Desk phone rings (because we didn't pick up our cell)-

You:	Hi, how's work going baby?
Me:	Good honey, what's up?
You:	Just wanna say hi...
Me:	Hi, baby...
You:	So what are you doing?
Me:	I'm working.
You:	Oh, right, are you having a good day?
Me:	Just busy.
You:	What do you want for dinner?
Me:	I don't care, something easy.
You:	What time are you going to be done?
Me:	I don't know, 5:30 maybe?
You:	5:30! I thought you said 5 this morning.
Me:	Yeah, well it's been a busy day, I gotta get this stuff done.
You:	Alright. Well do you think that you could stop by the store for me on the way home?
Me:	Sure, what do you need?
You:	You're in a bad mood. I'll just let you go!

Me:	Honey, I'm busy, that's all, I love you, please stop it...
You:	Stop what?
Me:	Getting all worked up...
You:	I'm not, you're the one that's being short.
Me:	I'm at work, that's all...
You:	Fine! Bye!
Me:	What is wrong honey?
You:	Nothing, forget it... bye...
Me:	Sweetheart?
You:	I'll just let you go back to your work (*this is said with as much sarcasm as possible*).
Me:	Baby please don't...

-Dial tone-

We almost always get at least one more phone call within the next hour.

"So, are you in a better mood yet?"

Look, it's very simple. Just try and limit the number of times each day that you talk to him, and I promise you'll soon find that the conversations are better. Talking frequently about nothing can kill a relationship fast. It causes unnecessary fights and pointless arguments. Your guy will begin to feel like you have absolutely nothing else going on in your life besides him, and that's a very bad thing.

It makes a guy feel like he's drowning. Now of course it's not true, right? You miss him. And of course you've got other things going on during your day. Usually they are important and crucial to making your life and your man's life comfortable. But if you're seriously calling your mother eight times a day, and your best wing girl ten times, plus add to that another twenty or so text messages, and

finally calling and texting your man for his own daily dose…
Well, I don't want to be the one to jump the gun and take his
side on things, but he may be on to something with that
whole "nothing else to do" thing. Let's find you a hobby! No
dear, Facebook doesn't count!

7. Smiley faces…

I know you won't believe me when I tell you this, but guys
don't care, and never will care, about those smiley faces. We
think that they're dumb and really over used. It's not cute,
it's more annoying, like popping your gum or saying "like"
or "you know" every three seconds. How annoying is that?
Stop with the smiley faces. If your guy sends them to you,
chances are that he also likes *Dancing With The Stars* and
The Bachelor too! And if that's the case, he may be in need
of some serious guy time. Encourage him to make some new
guy friends, ones that aren't complete pussies either. Btw, I
was a fan, but I stopped watching after she picked that
douche bag over Reid! I actually wrote her a letter, it was
short and sweet and it said,

   Dear Jillian,

   You're an idiot! What the hell was wrong
   with Kiptyn!
   By the way you look pretty today!

   Sincerely,
   Daryl

If you're wondering why it is that I didn't use a more current reference to *The Bachelor* it's because all the seasons have pretty much sucked since then.

8. Naked photos...

No matter what he says to you, or promises you, other people will see them. Posted on the Internet? Nah, most likely not. Shown to the boys though? Yep, it's almost a George Foreman guarantee.

9. Answering call waiting...

So explain this one for me. If you have voicemail, do you really need to click over to see who it is? I thought that's the whole point of having it? Apparently I'm wrong because as soon as there's another call, it doesn't seem to matter what's being discussed, you'll click over instantly. So for me, I have my own rule about it. I'll hang up as soon as someone clicks over. I don't want to wait, and I don't think that I should have to wait. I think it's rude to even assume that I would. As if I have all day free with nothing else to do but wait around until you have time to come back and finish our talk. If we're in a serious conversation and it's interrupted by, say, I don't know, a dancing baby, well that's one thing. I'd understand that. Dancing babies are fucking awesome.

All this talk about creating perfect babies through genetic engineering research and cloning procedures, but never once do you hear anybody talking about creating babies that can dance their little pink asses off? It's always about picking an eye color, having all ten fingers and no diseases. Who cares about that shit? I want a baby that can pop, lock and drop it! I want her to be able to Dougie, and then teach me. I want YouTube gold right out of the womb! A dancing baby is one thing to stop an important conversation for. You choosing to say, "hold on a second..." with no dancing baby, is another.

10. My final rule for cell phones is all about the "When..."

When is it ok? And when is not ok? When exactly are the right and wrong times for you to use your cell phone? If you do more than seven of these on a regular basis, well I know I've never actually met you before, but chances are pretty good that you're a complete ASSHOLE...

While we're driving in the car together - **not ok**
While at a restaurant for dinner - **not ok**
At my parents' house for a holiday - **not ok**
In our bed - **not ok**
At church on Sunday - **not ok**
At the gym - **not ok**
Out for breakfast with friends - **not ok**
While someone is speaking to you - **not ok**
Sitting at a live program - **not ok**
In a public bathroom - **not ok**
At a funeral - **not ok**
During a first encounter with someone new - **not ok**
In a meeting - **not ok**
While driving - **not ok**
During any meal - **not ok**
Going for a walk - **not ok**
On vacation on a beach - **not ok**
During a class - **not ok**
At the library - **not ok**

While a child is trying to show you something-**not ok**
Anytime it may annoy someone else - **not ok**
Anytime you're sure that you won't be bothering
anybody - **Yes, ok**

Got it? Good, I'm glad we cleared that up. ☺

Section Four- Phone Self Control

Look, all this stuff is going to take time. It's not a simple overnight fix. The guy that you're dating right now might not even care about this sort of stuff, and most likely he does some of it himself. It's still relevant though, and worth working on, and let me remind just you why that is; it's because by this time next year, you may not even be together. He may leave you before you even finish reading this book. God willing anyway, for your sake.

Maybe I'm wrong though? You have been learning something through all of this, right? So maybe this time around you'll leave him on your own. Well, when you finally do start over again, you'll need to rid yourself of all your worst dating habits in order to have a fighting chance.

How can I say something like that? It's because I know that there's something better out there for you. You know it, too. You wouldn't have made it this far through the book if you were really content in your current relationship.

The thing is bad habits are usually bad across the board. You'll need to start working on breaking them now or by the time you have your own kids, they'll follow your example. I know that right now this all seems pretty far-fetched (we're talking about a little thing, as simple as cell phone etiquette) but it will carry over to the other areas in your life. Trust me on that.

If you can't even give up a few bad phone habits now, how in the world do you expect to lose the baby weight when the time comes, or stop cursing when you have little monsters of your own running around the house? You need to pick out a few bad habits now and slowly start to trim off the fat. For example, take texting at the movies. Sounds like no big deal, right? But it really is, and here's why:

What starts out as a harmless behavior, slowly, but surely, will become your bad habit. See the problem is that bad habits are hard to shake, like herpes, ex-girlfriends or Nickleback (enough already, seriously Nickelback, that's enough out of you). Now with a thing like texting at the movies, it's not the texting as much as it's the deep down complete disregard for other people around you. And, like herpes (or Nickelback), it spreads. People will think that it's okay to do because they see that you think it's okay. It's just like when people have friends who curse a lot. Soon they find themselves beginning to curse more and more as time passes; I'm telling you that's no good, fuck that fucking shit!

Your bad habits will be passed on to your kids without you even trying to do it. They'll watch you, and they'll learn, and before you even know it, your kids will suck, and they will be little assholes too, and most likely, they'll have no clue as to why (just like you). You've got to push yourself to realize that other people are very much affected by your own actions. Your bad habits aren't only going to be yours. People share their bad habits. From sleeping in late to being overweight to texting at the movies, we've all got a few. So what bad habits will you bring to a relationship? Be careful because bad habits are learned, shared, practiced and eventually perfected. Only you can help yourself break out of this messy cycle. I'll give you my best example of people and how dumb they can be when it comes to bad habits, and maybe it will strike a chord for you.

The Big Mac

Yep, the Big Mac. Quite possibly one of the single worst food options ever invented. Is it even debatable just how bad they really are for you? Knowing this, I want you to answer a question for me:

Would you ever eat a Big Mac every day for a month straight? Well of course you wouldn't (unless you're Morgan Spurlock). How about every day for three months? Of course not! But WHY? They do taste good, and they're very affordable. I'm not talking about if you were a four hundred pound person with a very serious food problem. I'm talking about the everyday, fits-into-her-clothes-reasonably-well you. Why wouldn't you do it?

You wouldn't do it because you know just how bad they are for you. It's all very simple. The idea of eating something like that every single day seems insane to most people. Yet, those very same people who can agree with me on that statement, some of them anyway, and some of you, still smoke cigarettes. At some point people really don't care what their habit does to them.

Look, don't feel too bad, cigarettes are probably the most brilliantly and heavily marketed product ever. However, they're also the single most dangerous product ever sold to the general public. There's no disagreement about that one either, yet people still continue to smoke.

Why? Because it's an addiction? Maybe. Well of course that's a part of it, but that's a very simplistic excuse. It starts out as a routine, as a habit. Habits often become addictions. Good habits and bad habits alike. You get used to doing something over and over again, and soon it becomes normal to you. Normal then becomes the routine, and before you know it, bam, you have a full-blown addiction, and it can be to anything; food, exercise, drugs, cheating, sex, even

Big Macs, and at some point there's no thought required at all.

Cell phones just happened to be the topic of this chapter, texting while driving, talking while dining, it's all about the same thing: Bad habits that get worse and worse over time. Soon it becomes just the way that you do things. Most common relationship problems stem up from bad habits too. You're never taken out to dinner, so now you've become used to it. You're always on top during sex, and now it's become routine for you. He always pays for everything, and now it's not even special anymore (to you or him), it's just normal. So do your very best to spot the good and bad habits in your own relationship, and once you see them, start trimming the fat off the bad ones.

Obligation calls...

Taking obligation calls is the phone habit that absolutely takes the cake. Not good cake either, like red velvet, but stupid cake like lemon, or marble, or fruit...

These are the phone calls that we'll make to you, and take from you, because it's so much easier than just telling you that we don't really feel like talking right now. You've been crystal clear on your feelings about this. It's the same every time, for every single guy. From the very start of a relationship, girls will set their rules for phone time.
Guys are for some reason drawn right into it. Helpless, and without much protest, we submit. By week two we've given up all hope of ever having it be reasonable again. We've come to the conclusion that we're now your phone slaves until you tell us otherwise. Maybe I'm overreacting just a bit. After all, talking is nice, and communicating is important to any relationship. I'll also admit that I do appreciate the courtesy of checking in. I just wonder though, where does having zero trust in him and maybe a border line obsession fit into the equation? The need to talk ten times a day, everyday? Every single day?

In the morning, before work, at lunchtime, before your meeting, maybe a Facebook message after that, on the drive home, then at the grocery store! It's enough already!

The problem is that when I finally decide to grow a pair and skip out on one of those daily, must-happen calls, you go absolutely fucking crazy! And when out of town traveling for work, it's what I'd imagine being on parole would feel like. Even calling in just a single minute late is punishable by a guilt so thick, even a Catholic priest would be like, "Jesus fucking Christ girl, settle down!"

"Call me before you go to bed, ok?"
"Call me when you get up please."
"Just call me when you leave work."
"Will you call me when your meeting gets out?"
"You're going to call me right?"

You want to know what you're doing? You're acting just like our mothers. You might as well be wiping snot from our nose and using spit to get the jelly off our face because that's how we see you. It's not even that we don't want to talk to you. Most guys (myself included) love having a girl to call and say sweet dreams to. It's the simple fact that we don't have a say in the matter that makes us crazy. So we submit, not out of love for you, but out of fear. Fear of the evil you! We're afraid of the wrath we'd endure if ever you were to find out, truth be told, that we'd be completely fine if we didn't talk to you everyday.

-Caution: This next part is a secret, don't fuck me over, I'm trusting you!-

Your guy, husband, fiancé, boyfriend, lover, whatever he is to you, will not admit to most of this shit. He'd rather avoid having you huff and puff around for the next week, so he'll skip the chance to actually have a simple talk with you, which could make life better for you both. This, by the way, is your fault! Well actually, it's more likely your mother's fault. You learned from a very young age that pouting and acting like your feelings are hurt will get you all kinds of attention.

"Baby, honey, sweetheart, what's wrong?"

So you'll do it whenever the time calls for a serious power move on your part. Look, I would do it to if it worked for me, so I can't really blame you. Even if you don't think that you do this, trust me, you do. Shit, my mom even does this. In fact, I've even seen my grandma do this to my grandpa! Again, this is something that starts when you're young. We teach our little girls to be dramatic, and our little boys to be stone cold. To the little boy with a scraped bloody knee it's:

> "You're okay, stop crying, I said stop crying, now go back and play."

To the little girls it's:

> "Honey come here, tell Mommy what happened, where does it hurt baby?"

If you can break free of this (like I said though, my mom still does it) you'll begin to see how much easier things can be without all the theatrics. See, you're ready to take the stage at a moments notice, and he's ready to have no opinion on anything, and try to keep things as calm as he can at all costs. So because of this, it won't really do you any good to go and start badgering him until he finally breaks down and admits that I'm dead on about this shit, or even worse, until he says whatever it is, that he already knows you need to hear to let it go. I suggest that instead, you shock him by being different today. So simple, but yet so easy! Then you can feel free to thank me or send me a small gift when you two are still married ten years from now (if it's wine, I like red, not white) but either way trust me on this one, I'm right.

Seven

My Faceland...

You knew this one was coming didn't you? I've been waiting to write about this for about three chapters now. I got even more excited about it, when I recently received a random friend request on Faceland at about 2:30 in the morning. It was from my ex-girlfriend's mother, who by the way is over fifty-five years old! Thank God she didn't poke me.

We've started the great fall. Max out your credit cards, cancel your gym memberships, and, while you're at it, tell them to go ahead and super size it. Fuck it. We ain't walking away from this one. This online stuff is a gift and a curse. While it's nice to find old friends, acquire a sheep for your farm, and have someone whacked by the mafia, the downside is that we now have clear and substantial evidence that almost every girl online is truly in love with herself.

Once upon a time, when you liked a pretty girl, even if you had some sneaking suspicion that she thought very highly of herself, at least the possibility still remained that you could be wrong. But now it's well documented through the 2,134 photos that she's posted of herself online. The online social sites have created this crazy place for people to meet each other, without having to meet. Talk to each other, without ever having to speak. And worst of all, stalk each other, without ever disturbing a fly.

So you'd think, knowing all this, girls would be ten times more cautious and selective about sharing their personal information. Unfortunately, it seems the exact opposite is happening. Even employers have caught on to the benefits of Facebook stalking. They've now made it a point to look up their prospective employees before they'll commit to hiring them. And why? Well, we can't very well have a half naked, "Wasted Face Cathy" running our sales team, or a "Keg Stand Kenny" being responsible for the company's profit books, now can we?

Let's try and be a little more objective though, there is a greener side to this. Now you can take a peek into someone else's world and see if the real version of them is a good fit for you, or not. Let's just say for an example that you don't like to drink that much. Well then the girl who has a bottle in her hand in half of her photos is probably not the right choice for you. If you're a jealous type girl then the guy with tons of pretty girls commenting on his page every twenty minutes, might not be the best choice either.

When did we decide that Facebook was going to replace our local mall? Kids are supposed to hang out at the mall, it's an important American tradition! You'd get dropped off on a Saturday morning, sporting zits and bed head, so you could wander around and act awkward all day. That's how it's supposed to go! No more Orange Julius, no more tasty little bourbon chicken samples either[*]. The malls are quieter now than ever before because today's kids are off somewhere staring into a computer screen at their computer friends.

Let me just put it out there now and say that I feel young people (by young people, I mean children) have absolutely no business being online, at all. Get them a fucking book to read! If they need to look something up for school, I'll still offer you the same suggestion: get them a fucking book to read! You know what's so great about a book? It can't send you photos of its penis, or try to meet up with you for an afternoon rape.

Why do children need to be online? For what reason? My last girlfriend's little brother had a MySpace at age nine! Which of course meant that all his little school friends had one too. I'm not trying to be the old man in the room, but I do feel strongly about this one. The younger that kids are when they start getting online, the more fucked up they'll likely be, especially by the time they reach a dating age. How will they ever be able to build healthy relationships with people when most of their friends have existed only online? That's really the most negative part about an online anything. It keeps people from living their real lives.

---

[*] It's a fact that the youth of America is the most impressionable generation to market to. So how are the nice Chinese people supposed to get young Americans hooked on their low grade chicken disguised with fattening sauces if there are no kids scouring the mall for free samples?

I did the MySpace thing, and of course I have a Facebook now. Both of them served their purpose I can't deny that. The first time I heard about MySpace I was traveling on a music tour with a female pop singer for my job. No, sorry you don't get to know who it was. She has nothing to do with this story. I've always traveled around for work, and because of that, I knew people living just about everywhere. The only thing that sucked about traveling, was that it made keeping in touch with people very difficult. Of course it became so much easier with the birth of all these social websites, and for that alone, I'm very grateful.

When I first got a MySpace I didn't even think to look up anybody who was truly close to me. After all, I already spoke with those friends regularly. I instead looked up all the people who I had a difficult time keeping in touch with. Almost all of them were from other states or countries. I honestly don't think I had even one friend on there from where I lived. My friends from the music tour were on MySpace way before I was, and they kept insisting I get one because it was the easiest way of letting people know where I'd be as I traveled around the country.

So I got one. I'll save you the long history lesson.

Facebook soon followed (once only for college kids, now available for anybody with fingers) and then, like most hot trends, things got a bit carried away. What was meant to be a fun communication tool had soon become the very best way for people to *not* have to talk to one another. Very strange. Instead of talking, it actually became a personal billboard for people to show off their most superficial sides to one another.

Look at my body, look at all my friends, look at my car, look at my cat, look at my other cat, look at my kids, me, me, me, me.

Girls, I'm sorry to say, took the whole social media thing hook, line and sinker. They now had their very own digital scrapbook, one that everyone could see. Girls always cared more about this type of stuff though. I remember when we got our yearbooks in high school, I couldn't have cared less if someone signed my book; not the girls though, they ran around school filling up every fucking page.

"Sign my book! Wanna sign my book? I saved you a page!"

"Keep in touch"
"Stay cool forever"
"Have a good summer"
"You're a really nice guy! Love, Lisa xoxo."
"You're so funny"
"Sorry I cheated on you…"

And so on…

So of course it's no huge shocker (drink) that this became a major thing for young girls everywhere. The idea of having a place to share all your photos and leave your friends little notes was all very high school actually. And just like with high school, it quickly became a popularity and status contest.

"How many friends can I get?"
"How many people will wish me a happy birthday?"
"How many guys wanna fuck me?"

Also, just like in high school, it became the perfect place for bitchy, snobby girls to be mean to one another. Don't worry though ladies, guys soon followed suit with their own bullshit. They could now hit on a pretty girl without ever having to worry about the fear of rejection. They also found it a great place to adore themselves too. Do you have abs bro? Well now you have the perfect place to show them off, and if you have the unfortunate problem of living in Michigan, which sucks, where the ab season is particularly short, no worries brother, because now thanks to Facebook you can have your abs in your profile picture all year long! Poor Michigan.

Girls, not to be outdone, had entire albums dedicated to bikini photos. Where do I even start? Truly one of the great mysteries of women, one that even after countless relationships I can't fully explain. How come every time a girl has to change out of, or into a top, she'll say something like,

> "Turn around please,"
> Or
> "Hey, don't look, I'm changing!"

Yet, the bikini, which is the exact same thing to a guy's eyeballs as underwear, is considered fine? How can one of them be embarrassing, yet the other is no big deal?

Most girls, not all of them maybe, but for sure the skinny ones, have at least one photo album up on Facebook, where they put their bikini photos. It's either in the "Lake Norman Sandbar Album" or the "Spring Break Album." Could be their "Summer Fun Album!" Whatever the fuck they call it, it's up there for the whole wide world to see.

All right, you're at the lake, and you want to remember it for-ev-er. Ok, I get it. So maybe you take a few photos, and then you take a few more just in case. But why would you need to post all twenty of them online? It's not always at the lake, either. How about the ones of you at the pool party, or at the Hard Rock in Vegas? Why would you put up the Halloween photos where you're dressed as a vampire stripper? What about the ones from the pimps and hoes party where you're basically half naked? I truly can't wrap my little brain around it. What's the objective here?

Is it just to have some memories from that day? Maybe because you're not ashamed of your body, you figure why the hell not? I mean there must be a good reason that girls want to have so many of their bikini photos up for all to see.

If I'm out wake boarding and someone takes photos, my shirt will most likely be off. If I'm at a pool party, I'd say I most likely would be running around without a shirt too. So let's say that a bunch of these photos were taken of me. How about we go even further and pretend that it was with my own camera (which would never happen by the way). Now I'm back home at the computer with a major decision to make. Which ones should I upload? Well definitely the ones that I look good in, I get that, but why would I ever need to post twenty or more photos of myself without my shirt? Is there any reason at all past pure vanity? What would you think of a guy who had taken the time to upload over twenty photos of himself without his shirt on? He's a total douche bag, right? What if it was your own boyfriend who was doing it and you saw that earlier today he uploaded ten new photos of himself, all of them shirtless? What if they were of him at the gym?

Girls can't be at dinner, the pet store, work or wherever, without constantly snapping photos of themselves.

Guys see this as a huge turn off, and I'll tell you why. The reason isn't because you're doing the whole self-paparazzi thing, which is super annoying by the way, but it's that you lack the self-confidence to support that behavior in the first place. It would be one thing if you snapped photos all day long of yourself and really believed that you were pretty. True, it would still be completely self-absorbed behavior, but at least it would be fitting behavior to go along with the ego. Most times though, we still have to deal with the insecure whiney:

> "I hate my eyebrows!"
> "My hair is gross."
> "I want bigger boobs."

Where is all that self-confidence that warrants taking over two hundred photos of yourself during a single weekend? That's the part that guys really don't understand. We're suppose to be gentlemen, to treat a lady like a lady, but it's a tall order when he can show all his buddies what you look like in your underwear simply by logging in. And yes, girls do look the same in a bikini as they do in bra and panties. Don't believe me? Ask any guy. Shit, ask your father! I'm repeating myself now, but let's end this with one question. If guys are sex crazed, boob-obsessed animals, and a girl decides to post several pictures of herself basically in only underwear on her SpaceBook page, what's the message that I'm supposed to take from that?

We're in a Relationship... I Think.

Beyond the entire photo mayhem is the binding "relationship status." Single, it's complicated, married, dating... so many fucking options. Nothing is worse for a guy than finding out on Facebook that he is, in fact, dating you. Two dates in, and already you've got him listed as the one you're "in a relationship with." As soon as you two have a fight, the status is immediately changed to "it's complicated" until things are later resolved. It's crazy that people really stress out over it.

-"I thought that we were dating, but your Facebook says that you're still single, so I guess not?"

-"How about you change your status first and then I'll change mine."

-"So, I think that they're broken up because two days ago her status said 'In a Relationship' and now it doesn't!"

-"I know this is silly, but can you please change your relationship status to include me? My friends keep asking what we are."

-"I don't list my husband on there because people already know that I'm married!"

The fact that you can even list who you're in a relationship with is hilarious to me. Doesn't the person that you're with already know that they're with you? Don't all your real friends (or anybody that truly matters) already know whom you're dating?

So, who then is it really up there for? Hmmmm...

I guess it's on there for all the people that you don't know? The whole idea is beyond ridiculous. If you're really in a serious relationship and it's one that you truly care a lot about, Facebook offers nothing but problems for it. Why would you ever want to invite any extra-added stress to your relationship? Relationships are hard enough already without you including all 2,135 of your online friends to join in.

Of course you do realize that the book you're holding in your hands has its very own Facebook page, and I have a personal one as well, so yes, this whole chapter is kind of hypocritical, I'll admit that. I like to look at people's profiles, and search through all of their photos. It's a very voyeuristic type thing. It feels sneaky. I like it! Can you imagine though, if every time that you looked at someone's page or at their photos, Facebook sent out a little message to them? Man, we'd all be fucked!

> To: Me
> From: Facebook
> Subject: New profile footprint.
>
> 3:10PM: Brian just read through your comments.

> To: Me
> From: Facebook
> Subject: New profile footprint.
>
> 9:30PM: Katie just looked at your photos... again.

To: Me
From: Facebook
Subject: New profile footprint.

1:15AM: Bob just spent over 30 minutes looking through your past 100 status updates, and flirted with the idea of sending you a friend request.

To: Me
From: Facebook
Subject: New profile footprint.

Tim has now viewed your album titled "Spring Break," for the fourth time today, at 3, 4 & 5AM and then again at 9AM... P.S. You don't really know Tim, but he may have slept with that girl Carrie whom you also don't know but are "friends" with anyway. You accepted him because he kind of looked familiar at 2AM Saturday morning.

Leaving comments and tagging photos, blocking people and stealing your lover's password, it's a wild place online. At the end of the day, thank goodness it's only an online life. You can end it with the simple click of the button. It's that easy. You can walk away and nothing really changes. No one looks for you, no one cries for you. There will be no ribbons tied around trees for you or burning candles melting on steps. There are so many people online now that nobody will even know you've gone missing. It's okay though because it's not the real you anyway. Not even close. The online you and the real you wouldn't even recognize each other at the grocery store, not even if you both happened to be there buying Stouffer's French Bread Pizza (yes, it's a Dane Cook reference). The online you is a super-hero of sorts, one with special powers that can say things without hearing how they sound and hurt people without ever seeing the real pain.

Everyone's signed on for the thrill of it all. My aunts and uncles are on Facebook, 9-year-old girls have profiles, and now even people's house pets. I'm not quite sure how they log in though. It's true that being able to send out a message at a moment's notice to your friend that lives on the other side of the country is a great thing, but there is also a huge downside to it. It has all become way too impersonal.

Taking over at the place where emails and instant messaging left off are the social networking sites. A new idea, much easier and simpler to use, a fun way to connect to everybody whose name you can almost, kind of, sort of remember. They provide the taste without any of the substance. Kind of like those soy crisps. The idea is that they can replace real potato chips. Well they can't, and not just because they suck, but because they're not real potato chips! Sometimes you just need the real thing to feel satisfied.

A Christmas card will always be more meaningful than an email and a handshake always beats out a wall comment. A hug will always feel better than a "miss you" message and a poke can never replace a kiss. A status update will never be the same as hearing your real friend's voice.

Spend some quality time offline, and when your "friends" ask you where you've been? Tell them, you've decided to live your life... aay yay, aay yay, aay yay...

We miss you T.I.

Eight

Guy Space

Guys only have a few simple needs in life to be completely and truly happy. You may think that you already know what these are. Well do you? It's long been believed that guys are simple creatures and require only food, sex and the occasional beer to be as happy as an ocean clam.

Sigh...

If only it were that simple! I won't be able to tell you absolutely everything that your man needs, because I don't know him. I can tell you that the most important thing is not what's between your legs. It's really no wonder that there's so much confusion about all this stuff. Whenever so-called relationship experts describe "men," they talk about us as if we're this wild pack of animals, roaming the wilderness, scratching, biting, fucking and operating without any self-control; slaves to our primal instincts. To hear them tell it, all that men apparently require are life's most basic essential needs:

> Food, sex, air, water, good health and maybe more sex...

If you want to get fancy you could throw in a job that he cares about and a personal relationship with God, but that, along with all the rest of the stuff, is already a given. No big shocker there (If you're playing the "WJNTY" drinking game... that's another shot!) The real problem with that list is this:

> A: It's dumb.
> B: It doesn't involve you (minus the sex part).

Let's say, just for the hell of it, that list is everything that men do need. Now what? What happens if your man's list is missing some, or worse, all of those things?

"Well, at least he has me. Isn't that enough?"

Women will often make the mistake of believing that *they* are the missing link, the reason, or even the magical answer to all of their guy's problems, when actually, you can't really do much to help him out at all. The only person who can change any of those things for him, is him. Sure, you can offer support and even try to steer him in the right direction, but in the end, you will not be able to do it for him. Trying to change things in someone else's life, over which you have absolutely no control, is as effective as trying to solve an algebra equation by chewing bubble gum. It just doesn't work… but trust me on the sunscreen (if you got that last reference, you're fucking awesome). Anyhow, the point is it's a complete waste of your energy and time.

However, what *is* worth your time is finding out which things you do have the power to change, and focus on those instead.

What things are these, you ask?

We are talking about you: the way that *you* treat him, how *you* act, and how *you* react to things that he says and does. See, the way that *you* behave towards your man, is really where all the answers lie. The answers to all those worries and wonders you have about your guy:

> Will he cheat on me?
> Will he leave me?
> Is he ever going to marry me!?
> Why is he so obsessed with anal?

Do you want these answers? Good, because they lay in your soft little hands. It's all up to you. Don't let them slip through those pretty French manicured tips.

It's a lot of pressure to have the success of your relationship all depend upon you and your actions, and it is a big responsibility. I know that it doesn't seem fair, but do you really think "we" don't understand? Try knocking out the rent one month. Fuck it. Tell you what, how about we start even smaller than that, how about you just pay the light bill…

God, I wish I had a vagina.

Guys Are All the Same!

Guys do think alike, especially when it comes to the important stuff, or rather the stuff that's important to you. Any girl
out there who wants to find a good boyfriend and keep him
for herself, and then hopefully have that boyfriend become
her husband, should be paying very close attention to this
chapter. The reason isn't just so you can learn how to be the
perfect little wife for him, or learn how to do absolutely
everything in your power to make him a happier man (although you should be aiming dead on for both of those). It's
because,

PAUSE... Gasp, did I just hear some scoffing from
you?

Look, if after reading that you just rolled your eyes,
huffed, or made that weird girl click sound with your mouth
(the one guys can't do), you know, that noise girls make
when they swivel their heads around and say "Oh no he
di'int" I need you to simmer down right now and listen with
your eyes, very closely to me...

The reason is this:

If you aren't willing to try and be the very best version of yourself for him, or even worse, you don't want to
try, then there's really no point in being together in the first
place. The whole idea is supposed to be that what makes *him*
the happiest guy in the world is making your day just a bit
brighter and a little bit better than it started off. The same
should go for you. If you two don't have that, you're both
probably with the wrong person. I mean it. Look, it can happen to the very best of us, just like it did for young Rose
DeWitt Bukater.

Sometimes the guy you're with, well, he just sucks. And then you bump into a cute boy named Jack Dawson, and so what the hell? You fuck him in a Model-T Ford on a sinking boat... these things happen.

Rose said it best:

"I'd rather be his whore than your wife."

OH SNAP!

What a great line, and what a truly great love story and one we can all learn from.

What We Learned From Titanic...

Remember Rose? She was a 17-year-old rich girl and was already set to be wed when she took a ride on the grandest ship in the world. It was an arranged marriage though, and she *so* hated Caledon. Well, guess what? So did I. He was a major dick. But what did it matter because he was still her fiancé. What's a girl to do?

Try and jump off of the damn boat, that's what! How could she have stayed? She truly hated him. He was really controlling and old. Furthermore, he treated her like she was his little daughter. As for Rose's mother Ruth? Well, she pretty much sucked, too. They both treated her like she was an infant who couldn't do anything by herself, a silly helpless child. Well guess what? Rose was ready to show them! In her attempt to act like a mature grown up, she decided she would kill herself by jumping overboard into the icy water below. Well, she fucked that up too. But, luckily for her, Mr. Jack Dawson from Chippewa Falls, Wisconsin, was lingering near by (he's a fucking lingerer, bro), and he was able to save her clumsy ass.

She was very grateful for their chance meeting as one could imagine because not only were they close in age, but he also saved her from pulling a straight up Natalie Holloway... (Hey, calm down you. Like you even knew that girl. Look, don't go getting wasted face with crazy Dutch boys on your vacation, we've been over this before.) All right, so anyhow, Rose decides that Jack is much more interesting than Caledon, and much younger, and so she takes off all her clothes for him. Noooo, not for that reason! Get your mind out of the gutter! She did it so that he could draw pictures of her, just like he used to do with the street girls back in France. I believe it was with Cleo, a one-legged French hooker? I'm not positive though it's been a while since I've seen the movie. But either way, it was a brilliant move. Jack was fucking smooth I'll give him that.

So she gets completely naked except for her crazy bling necklace, (remember it from the Britney Spears music video?) the heart of the sea, or of the ocean? It doesn't really matter. The point is, that fucking rock was HUGE! She wanted to wear it just to spite Caledon. It seemed, even at 17, she fully understood that getting naked for another man while wearing a gift from her fiancé was going to ruffle some feathers. Classy girl. Anyhow, now that she'd been naked, and Jack had seen the full monty, what else was there left to do?

Exactly... but where to go? They were only 17 and they didn't have a private room. Jack was staying in the 3rd class cabins, and they couldn't do it down there- way too many rats. Well, in true teen hookup fashion, they found their way into the back seat of an automobile, (William Carter's "Renault traveling car" to be more accurate). And now the boy who didn't have two pennies to rub together was literally making it count. Somehow he nailed the rich girl in the backseat of this car, which was fine by her because she was hell bent on slumming during her vacation anyhow! How do I know that she was slumming? She told us, remember...

"I'd rather be his whore than your wife..."

Damn Caledon, you just got served again, that's twice now in one chapter!

Now most "whores" have condoms with them, which would have been good because I'm guessing that if trusty Jack didn't have two pennies, he definitely didn't bring condoms along with him either!

No need to worry though because they'd end up spending the next four hours in freezing ice cold water, which everyone knows works way better than a coat hanger.

What, too far? Sorry, my fault, I meant better than a flight of really steep stairs.

So this was the great love story that set box office records world wide before Cameron's giant blue Smurfs knocked Titanic out of the number one spot. Figure that one out. Score one for FernGully!

Anyway, teen girls would be able to say whole heartedly that it was their very first "real love story." You know, minus cartoons and animals. Way before "Team Edward and Bella," there was Jack and Rose. Every bit as romantic of course, but maybe not the best love lesson for teens.

Have unprotected sex, strip for strangers on vacation, cheat on your fiancé and learn how to spit just like a man. And if you do all that, well, you'll get a rock even bigger than the one that Kobe had to give to his wife for sticking it in that little white girl in Colorado (silly Kobe). Oh yeah, and a poor, dead, homeless dude's baby.

-The End-

The good news is that you're not Rose DeWitt Bukater. It's so much easier for you, especially because you're:

A. Not on a sinking ship.
B. Hopefully already with the right person.

Being with the wrong person can have deadly conesquences. Rose ended up getting Leo killed, I mean Jack, because she was with the wrong person. This set off the whole fucking chain of events, sort of like the butterfly effect. That's probably why they hit the iceberg, too. Arranged marriage or not, if you find yourself at the point where you're really thinking about leaping off a boat into the icy ocean below, it's probably a little too late. You need to get out way before your relationship hits an iceberg and starts taking on water.

It's not supposed to be so hard. Or so dramatic. Deep down, people know this. That's why you're always hearing them say, "When you know, you just know." It's not some big cryptic *Da Vinci Code* type deal. It's simple, almost effortless. Just like those people who are insanely successful in business. They'll often say things like, "If you do something that you truly love doing, success comes easy. It doesn't feel like you're doing work at all."

The same can be said for relationships. It only becomes tons of work for you if you don't really love the person you're with. Maybe you feel that you do really love him, yet for some reason you two still can't seem to get it together. What's a girl to do then? Well, since *we* can only control the things that *we* do, let's start from there.

Are men difficult? Yes, if not impossible. But more often than not, it's going to be something that you've been doing that's making things even worse for the both of you.

If you're disagreeing with me right now, it's because you're way too stubborn and self-centered (just like your mother). How do I know this? Let's call it a gift. Most of the time it's the girl, not the guy, who needs to make only a few minor adjustments to get her impossible grumpy old man to become as docile as a cute, fuzzy koala bear. I know what you're thinking, "I want a man, not a fucking koala bear."

Fair point. But I'll have you know that real koala bears are not always the sweet, soft little bears that we've plastered all over our Trapper Keepers. No sir, they have sharp teeth and sharp claws, and they're to be absolutely feared when not behind the protected glass at a zoo. They can be angry little fuckers, those damn marsupials, and they even get chlamydia! I'm serious! Google it if you doubt me. It's fucking crazy right? In Australia they're often referred to as "drop bears" and they cause about as much trouble as alligators and snakes do down in Florida. However, they're said to be pretty chill and well behaved when you leave them alone. Let them be what they are meant to be, a koala bear, and you shouldn't have a problem.

Where am I going with all this? Well, the same thing can be said for men.

What's so great about men is that we're actually very easy to please. I'm not saying simple, don't make that mistake, that's television speaking. Men aren't horny, sports-obsessed cavemen who are afraid of diapers and housework. That's the sitcom Dad, and trust me, everyone's not Raymond! It's not a real thing. Real men are actually very complex just like you. Real men have feelings, too! Though it's fair to say that living their day-to-day lives, while fulfilling their typecast roles as the tough, testosterone-driven, hunter badass, doesn't really allow much time for it!

So I called this chapter Guy Space.* What does that really mean? It's about letting your guy be a guy. A common mistake that many girls make in their relationships is not allowing their guy any "guy space." The real tragedy of this is that most girls don't even realize when they're doing it.

---

* Guy Space: refers to his mental real estate or a lack there of. Space, which is needed for your man to function at his proper potential. More clearly stated it's the amount of space that your man needs or is allowed by you, to act, feel, live and love as a true man. Not always pertaining to mental space, it can also be a physical space. Example: I need some guy space! Where can I put my fucking toothbrush!?

My Little Pony Was a Badass, I Swear.

Think of a wolf out there somewhere in the wild.

I know! No, you're right, here we go again with the over-used typical male/wolf analogy thing, right? Room to roam, the need to get dirty and be around other wolves? I agree, it's no good. All right then, let's try it this way: think of a tiny pony, I mean what girl doesn't want her own little pony right?

I had My Little Pony toys when I was a little boy. Don't ask. I had an orange one that smelled of peaches, a blue one of some sort, and there was a white one with a rainbow on it, which had shiny pretty red hair, like O•P•I Red Red Rhine! The blue one had a thundercloud on it, I think. Were they supposed to be flying ponies? I seem to remember them all having wings. Anyway, they came with their very own little brushes so that you could comb their shiny manes.

The question you are all asking, is why did I have these? And why am I admitting to it? Um, well I'm not really sure, but they were mine, I do remember that. I also had a boy Cabbage Patch doll, and look, since I promised you this book would be honest, my brother had one as well (sorry Vincent). We even had a special drawer in our playroom with doll clothes in it. You know, so that we could dress them up in different outfits! Little army uniforms, football jerseys, shoes, tiny overalls and a train conductor's cap (my favorite). My parents were extremely relaxed in terms of their views of what toys were considered normal for little boys to play with. So I had a Cabbage Patch doll and some ponies, and maybe some scratch off nail polish that may have belonged to my little sister, before I stole it from her... no big deal, right?

Let's talk about something else please! How did we even get on this topic anyhow? Damn you Adderall. Oh that's right, the whole pony instead of the wolf thing. Fine, so my point is this: a little pony has a few basic needs in life, and these needs are nothing like that of your man. However, there are a few things, which, if you were to deny your little pony and force it to go without, well, it could really mess your little pony up. Men are the same in this regard.

For starters, a pony needs to be around other ponies, and it needs to be allowed to do pony-type things in order to feel like a "real pony." Eat hay, jump around, bite other ponies and so on. Sometimes, because they're very small, they tend to get insecure. Especially when they're around bigger horses- get the analogy? Because of this, ponies will require some extra love and encouragement to feel good about themselves. Just like with an insecure guy who doesn't have a body like Beckham or a Trump-sized bank account. But, most importantly, you have to let a pony be a pony to keep it happy. As soon as you try and treat your pony like a puppy, you'll start to have some major issues. Same goes with a man.

Who's My Big Strong Man? You Are! You Opened That Jar of Pickles So Good, Yes You Did!

Girls will often ask, "Why are some guys so jealous?"

It stems from having major insecurities about not feeling like "real men." See, most men really do need women, now more than ever before, in order to feel like true men. Though it hasn't always been that way. Once upon a time a man's daily life left no other choice than to be a *real* man. Basic everyday survival depended on it. We'll dig deeper into that in just a bit, the point is this: those feelings are still buried somewhere deep inside of him, and his daily life today doesn't offer him much of an outlet for it. The fact is that having sex with you twice a month and playing on his work's softball team just ain't cutting it dear.

This is why you see bar fights, steroid use and rampant cheating. It's all about Guy Space. This may sound a bit familiar in some respect to the movie called *Fight Club*. I have often told girls to watch that movie and focus on what it's actually saying instead of just drooling over Jared Leto and Brad Pitt. The whole movie is really about Guy Space, and it explains with great clarity what's going on today with your modern man. At some point we switched from being your protectors and providers to your listeners and cuddlers. There was bound to be a tipping point from all of this, and I believe that it's right now. You can only pretend to be something that you're not, for so long.

Not My Guy, He Loves Scrapbooking...

More delusions. My poor sweet girl. Ok look, here's the thing, just like with credit cards, your guy, believe it or not, does have limits. Sure, he loves being around you, and he may even share some things in common with you. But there is a point when enough is enough. A great example of this is, *How To Lose A Guy In Ten Days*. What made that movie so funny, to me, was that some girls really do act like that. Not all of them, of course, but more than you'd ever imagine. Guys, in turn, really do pretend that it doesn't bother them... at first.

Well, call me Mark Felt because I'm about to blow hard.

You're kidding me, right? Um... famous whistle blower from the FBI? Changed American political history forever? Jeffrey Wigand, Jennifer Long?

Seriously? Is *Twilight* the only fucking thing that you've read?

Well here's some late breaking news for you: Guys are nothing like vampires, and real guys would do almost anything to avoid arguing with a girl. Especially with the girl who's currently having sex with him.

Cat got your tongue? What that really means is: pussy got your tongue? Because guys will say, or not say, almost anything to keep from losing what little pussy they might be getting from you. Sorry for using the P-word, I thought cunt was too much.

It usually starts out as something small, like maybe watching your favorite TV shows. I'll tell you though, guys don't find McDreamy that dreamy. Or maybe it's having him run to the mall with you to grab some bare essentials? Swirl, swirl, tap, tap, is that right?

Look, in the very beginning of the relationship, guys make the mistake of doing those little things that they don't really like doing, just to please you. It starts out sweet and well intentioned, but then just like a dad who offers piggyback rides all the fake fun begins to wear off. You kind of go through the motions the first ten times, but now your daughter thinks that you love piggyback rides as much as she does, and she'll ask for a ride over and over again! Well, now that she's over sixty pounds, and you really haven't committed to that P90X yet, it kind of sucks.

It doesn't end with activities, either. In fact, this whole chapter is really about how guys don't communicate well (yes, it's our fault this time). Take something as simple as the bathroom shower. Seems like a boring place right? Well it was, until you brought over five shampoo bottles, two different conditioners, a box of tampons and a few luffas. What the fuck is a luffa anyway? And please tell me, why do you need more than one of them? Don't forget about that weird razor thing, the one that sticks to the shower wall. The tough part is, you asked him, and he most likely told you he was fine with it. Well, actually what he probably said was more like,

> "I don't care, just put some stuff under the sink if you want to."

Which really just meant for you to bring over a toothbrush and a hair tie thingy so that he doesn't always have to hold your hair back when you perform, um, your bathroom rituals. Most likely that's how it all started. But then just like a disease or Justin Bieber, it spread from there. From a cat to an ugly sweater, Keith Urban even sang a song about it! Girl shit is now everywhere: in his car, on the dresser, beneath the bed, of course under the sink, even in the hall closet. Don't forget about the ever-popular drawer, the one that he was nice enough to clear out for you.

The Drawer...

Every girlfriend knows that she's doing a good job when she's given her very own drawer. Now the obvious question is, why does it really matter? Is having some stuff around his house a big deal? It goes back to the whole "having limits" thing. A tough truck feels way less manly with tampons rolling around in its glove box. A boyfriend starts to feel like a husband with a bra drying on the doorknob and a pink toothbrush resting comfortably on the sink. It would be just fine if he *were* your husband. When he's just the boyfriend though? No way! He'll start to feel like he's losing control of the situation. And trust me on this, guys love to feel in charge like Charles! Even if he tells you that he doesn't really care about those things, believe me, he does.

Well why won't he admit it?

I'm glad you asked. It's simple really:

A.   He's afraid you will never play with his penis again.

B.   He's a weak pussy who's afraid of you! Is that really the kind of guy you want teaching your son how to be a man?

C.   You're not his wife yet. You're just the girlfriend that makes him think twice about ever having a wife.

D.   You're the girl willing to have sex with him and you let him put his penis in your mouth.

Sorry, I wish I had better news for you. If you want a relationship that lasts longer than Sammie and Ronnie, you're going to have to give him some space to be a man, plain and simple. You're also going to have to try and make him feel like "The Man."

Huh?

What do you mean, "What about you?"

Not right now. We'll get to that question in a bit. Stay focused.

Like I said earlier, lots of things have shifted now in our modern day relationships. It's not really your fault, but it *will* be if you don't get a handle on it. Everywhere you turn now things continue to get messier. Cheating is not frowned upon anymore; it's almost become completely acceptable, unless it's being done to you. Everyone seems to be doing it. Equally disturbing to me is now girls are treating their men just like girlfriends instead of treating them like men.

Way Back Before Old Spice...

Back in the day, guys didn't have such a hard time being guys. For starters, they acted like men. But they also looked a lot more like men. Even if we don't always look the part now, I promise you, there are still real men somewhere out there. I know that between all the manscaping and skinny jeans, we're starting to look like a bunch of Backstreet Boy, B-squad alternates. It's no wonder that guys are turning into complete pussies everywhere you look.

Bieber bangs and tiny dogs, spray tans and high-lighted tips? Marvin, please tell me! What the fuck is going on? When did we start to lose all our men? If I had to pin-point it to an exact location and time, I'd say it was for sure somewhere in the nineties, near a place called the Peach Pit in the California zip code of 90210. Dylan and that Brandon Walsh prick paved the way for tight jeans, hair gel and the "Seacrest" amount of neatly trimmed stubble. Real men had apparently gone away, maybe into hiding, because they were getting even harder to find than the point of one of those Tyler Perry movies.

Think of men like Kevin Costner, Burt Reynolds, Robert Redford, Sean Connery and Gregory Peck.

Those are the sorts of men that women want to drop their panties for. Not for all this smooth faced, bleached teeth, metro shit that's going on. It all has to stop. A man is supposed to be a man, and we're at risk of losing them all. Soon they'll be gone and all that will remain will be the left over, bed headed, spray tanned, soy drinking, fancy jean wearing, BBMing, tiny camera carrying, never been in a real fight, crying skinny little bitches.

The Last of the Man-hicans

No one will be around to change the oil in the car, no one to go downstairs and check out the scary noises in the dark. No one to turn the lights off in the garage and no one to kill those creepy spiders! You're in charge ladies. It's all up to you. What kind of man do you want? One better, what kind of man do you want teaching your son to be a man?

Other countries still have real men around, and we do too, but it's fading fast, like Tiger Woods' career. So do your part to help the cause. Keep your makeup in that purse and keep those tampons in your own damn car. While you're at it, why not let him be a naked man in the shower with a simple bar of soap? He'll get just as clean without having three different types of pretty berry-scented soaps in there for him to try. For God's sake woman, a bathroom is supposed to be for shitting and cleaning your body, not entertaining guests. Why does it have to smell like cinnamon cookies all the time? Why do we need a box of dried up leaves that smell of vanilla, but then you can't stand to see a single fucking leaf in our yard? Why do we have to decorate the room with seashells, when we don't live anywhere near the sea?

It's no wonder that girls get bored with their own men these days. None of the guys that girls even consider to be "hot guys" would be caught dead buying into that type of shit! Helping you pick out Easter bunny salt and pepper shakers or raincoats for your pugs? Do you really think Beckham, Pitt or Pattinson are at a Pier One right now looking at place mats for Thanksgiving? Fuck no they're not; they're out having sex with girls that are bored to death with their own boyfriends. Ok, just so I don't get sued, that last part was all made up (wink, wink). Remember, half of you reading this right now are with good guys. Good guys that would, and could, be great men if you'd only leave them alone long enough to act like one.

That Would be Grrreeaaat Ummmm Kay...

If your guy goes to work all day long, chances are good that he doesn't get much guy space there either. Maybe your guy's lucky and has a guy job.

What's a guy job you ask? Good question. How about what's not a guy job, that's easier...

If it includes meetings, ties, dress socks, shaving, Power Points, copy machines and answering emails, that's not a guy job.

So imagine this, by the time your poor guy finally gets off from work and gets back to his land of matching hand towels (that are never supposed to be used) and a fucking duvet cover with flowers on it, usually coupled with matching decorative pillows (that are also not supposed to be used), you start right in on him with a pointless update about your best girlfriend and her mind numbing bullshit. He listens because he loves you. Finally you toss in how hard it was to park at the mall earlier today, and how *he* really should have been driving that truck/big SUV that you begged him for. At the end of your very interesting story you ask if he remembered to pick up the milk. Oh shit, he fucked up again. He forgot to pick up the milk on the way home. While you're reminding him of this fact, he's already out to the car getting buckled back in, and this thought hits him like a shot to the heart, but it's too late: not only did he forget the milk, but he also hasn't had sex in almost two months and he hasn't watched a game since who knows when.

Once again, being a man is not on the list of activities for today, but there's still a small glimmer of hope because both *Extreme Home Makeover* and the new

Bachelor are on tonight. And before you fold those clothes
and wash your face, he hopes that with any luck, you might
even let him stick it in, if only for a second. It's a lonely time
to be a man, and worse to not feel like one in the first place.
If you have a sad feeling after that awful picture I've just
painted and you're wondering if your guy feels the same
way, I can offer you some advice.

Don't ask him. Instead, tell him tonight when you
see him that what you'd really like, more than even having
him come with you to the candle store event, is for him to go
out and visit with his friends this weekend. Watch for his
reaction and see what kind of girlfriend/wife you've become.
If he looks up at you like he is in trouble, or is being tricked,
you've got some major work to do. If he looks really scared
like he's done something bad, congratulations, you've now
become his mother.

One thing you need to remember is that you still
have your girlfriends (the ones you like and the ones you
don't), you have your mother, and now you have his mother
and his sister. Who does he have? His co-workers? Tell me,
when was the last time you really liked someone at work?

If you're thinking, "But he's a guy, he doesn't need
that, and plus he has me and the kids!"

Oh man, I feel just awful about this, I shouldn't
really be the one to tell you, but I guess I will. You might
want to go ahead and sit down for this.

Now listen to me…

You WILL become divorced. At least once. That's if
you haven't yet already. And you'll most likely lose him to a
woman who makes him feel like more of a man than you do.
Not a prettier woman, just a woman who's willing to give

him more guy space than you did. This could have been a-voided.

He doesn't need that? He has you and the kids!? What is this, fucking *7th Heaven*?

If it were just as simple as letting him shoot some pool or play with his tools, there wouldn't be much of an issue here. Some women really believe that. They believe that a guy cutting the grass in the yard counts as guy time. Guess what? I hate to keep saying it, but not all men are like television sitcom characters.

Some "real guys" like to read books, some like to write, and others like to hunt or do Sudoku puzzles. Some even like to go for runs, or drink coffee on the back porch alone, or (gasp) take baths. Believe me, the more you make him feel stupid or guilty for doing something that he enjoys, the more your relationship will start to remind him of a mother/son type deal. We love our moms of course, but having her nag us about absolutely everything stopped being cute after the eighteenth year of it. She always has an opinion (which will never change) and your mother probably does too! She didn't like our friends, our hair, our music or our choice in clothes.

"Don't waste your time with those baseball cards."

"Who plays video games anyway?"

"How come you don't choose better friends?"

"Is that your very best?"

"You need to work harder!"

Let's play a game. This one's for the guys reading. It's called, "Who said it, my mom or my wife/girlfriend?"

-Take your shoes off!
-Did you take the trash out?
-You said you were going to be home at 5.
-Don't use those towels, use the other ones.
-I thought you said you'd fix that.
-Is there anything you need ironed for to-morrow?
-Do we have milk?
-Is it cold in here? I'm cold.
-The basement is a mess, I thought you said that you'd clean it.
-Did you buy milk?
-Why are there so many remotes?
-You're watching sports, again?
-Why is the towel on the floor?
-Why isn't there any milk!?
-Put the lid DOWN!!!

Men do need women. Don't think for a second that we don't, but we also need other men around. We desperately need that lifeline to be able to feel like real men again.

Don't Worry Little Lady, I'll Fix Your Wagon...

You see, once upon a time our job was to be "The Man" and it was a great job to have. While we men were off doing that, you'd get to be "The Woman," and somewhere this all got off track. Way off track.

Our grandfathers used to rotate their own tires, put in their own spark plugs, do the timing on the distributor, adjust the points, grease the rods and so on. They'd take down the window screens and put up the storm windows. They'd fix the fences and paint the doors. They had a general custodial role in the home. They had a purpose to fulfill: to protect and serve the family, to be "The Man."

This is what's now missing in a man's life. Even worse, because of all our modern advances, there's even less for him to do. We have cars that can go 100,000 miles between tune-ups and combination windows so we don't have to put up the storm windows anymore. There's pre-finished siding and trim on the house so that painting is not required. All so that we have more time to relax. This just makes us feel irrelevant, and so we're tossed into the strange role of the companion, sensitive lover and friend. We've been robbed of being real men. Is this a woman's fault? No, of course not. But you do have the choice of feeding the problem or becoming part of the solution. Just like men, you need space to be women.

Women didn't used to have hobbies, mostly because they were busy being amazing women! Spending the day cooking, cleaning and mothering.

There are women who are reading this right now thinking,

"Fuck that, he wants us to go back to a time when women took care of men!"

Of course I do! Who wouldn't? Can you even explain that to me? How mothering, feeding and taking care of your family would ever be considered a negative thing? To mother your own children, instead of having some daycare or nanny do it for you, just so you can have another pair of True Religion jeans, or a nicer car, maybe a bigger house?

Women used to take pride in being the sole caretaker for their families, and rightfully so, because men really needed it, and so did the children. While men were out busy making the money to support the household, women were busy making that household into a home. Is there a nobler job anywhere in the world? A loving home is what's needed to become a great man or woman. Love, with support, mothering and guidance! Women took the role of mothering very seriously. Believe me, they weren't reading up on what Marilyn was wearing, or who Judy Garland was banging. They were way too busy being amazing women that you could admire. Their days were filled from morning to night with so much more than soccer games, vagina waxing and purses.

Amazingly, nowadays it's become a skill to be able to cook. Back then it was considered practically unthinkable not to be able to cook. Another thing, when did having nice things become more important than having nice kids?

The problem is, of course, that most women reading this will turn instinctively to the, "Well, what about the men?"

Sure, what about the men? Men should be held accountable for being real men, I agree with you. The fact is, behind every great man is an amazing woman. So what happens if there isn't an amazing woman behind him?

"Lots of women *have* to work, dick!"

That's true, they do. So who raises the babies? Who teaches them right from wrong? Who is the mommy then? Do you really think that children call out for the babysitter, nanny or day care teacher when they're scared? No, they call out for mommy.

Eight hours of work in a day for mom, plus sleep six to eight hours and then throw in a little TV, not to mention that "me" time, and what do we have left? Maybe, if you're lucky, an hour a day to be mom?

I'm not saying I have the answer, I'm just saying it's something to think about. Tell me one possession, one thing in your house, one fancy car, one handbag, that's worth more to you than spending time with your own children or husband.

I'm in Love With a Stripper

Look, it happens, but at the end of the day he'd rather have you think that he's sexier than the trainer, your neighbor or the clerk at the hardware store. You take that away from him and you'd better start using condoms. A man will only cheat on you when he's miserable, and he'll only be miserable when you withhold love. You won't fuck him because you don't feel like it, but then you get all heartbroken when he fucks her? You don't want to *have* to help boost his ego, but when the girls at his office do, you get upset?

Why do you think guys go to strip clubs? To see some boobs?

You have boobs.

For some sexy flirting?

You can do that for him too!

Because a $10 cocktail tastes that much better than a $4 one?

Please...

They only go there because the girls make them feel like real men. Sexy, powerful men. Even if it's only for a three and a half minute song. It's sad that men are willing to pay for something that their own wives could be doing for them for free.

Are you upset or angry? Maybe you think that what I've just said was complete bullshit? I promise you it's not. I just gave you the key to understanding men. I told you the deep dark secret. I just sold out every guy out there, and they all hate me now, but I did it for you and for them.

Nine

Listen, It's Not You, It's Me...

Breaking up. Is there really anything worse? Tummy aches, tears, puking and a pathetic version of yourself that's almost unforgivable. It doesn't matter which side of it you're on either, whether you're doing the break or being broken up with, it all pretty much sucks.

What's the worst part of a break up? Is it different for everybody?

Well that's kind of hard to pinpoint. I've been through some nightmares myself and while some of them seemed cleaner than others, they all ended up leaving some nasty scars.

It's kind of like being a drug addict who's trying to break away once and for all. Not just from the good stuff either, but also from the person you've used with. One of you is finally ready to get clean, to get your life back, your mind back, and yourself back. But that's easier said than done because the other person remembers fondly just how much fun using together really was and they can't begin to fathom how you'd ever consider giving that up. They're completely baffled that you don't see how much better things could be if you'd just use with them again,

Just one last time...

Please... one last time...

What do you mean no? You never really loved me did you?

It can be a hazy time when you're using. The details aren't always crystal clear. Or the memories for that matter. One thing that sucks in particular is that you're never entirely positive who's at fault, or who gets to hate who. The past is a huge fucking blur, like a bad car accident where everybody has a different version about what went down. It was a blue car, right? No wait, was it was green? I know we slid because of the rain, or maybe it was sunny out? All that doesn't really matter, because the point is, there was a bad wreck!

Whenever a good friend is going through it, you suddenly become an expert in heartbreak warfare, trained in field ops, enemy tactics and the rules of engagement, both domestic and foreign. All your expertise goes to waste, and it's really a crying shame because you're positive that you could help out, if you could only get them to listen to you. But they won't, because they've been on that stuff now for so long, it's of no use. At this moment in time they've gone completely insane, and there's nothing to be done about it but just sit and wait it out.

Waiting is the worst part of any break up. I mean, I know I said before that I couldn't pinpoint it, but it's all coming screaming back to me now. Waiting is definitely the worst part of any break up.

Waiting...

-To move on.
-To get back together.
-For the phone to ring.
-To listen to that voicemail that was just left.
-Until it's safe to go back to "our" spots to eat again.
-To hear them say *they* were wrong.
-To hear "I'm sorry."
-To forget what color their car is.
-To feel like living again.
-To have sex and not feel sick after.
-To have your mother not bring him/her up during the holiday discussions.
-To go on a date where you don't think a-bout him/her the entire time.

I could go on and on.

Even if you're the one who's doing the leaving, it doesn't get much easier. Guilt, mixed with some heavy doubt, is a motherfucker yo, trust me on that one. Some days you can't even remember why it was that you wanted to be "clean" in the first place. Every memory from your past with that person is given a nip and tuck. In your own head you've carefully edited out all the gory details. You play it over and over again until you remember your "new" and much improved version as the real thing, and soon you begin to forget about the one that actually had taken place.

Everything is re-mastered just like BluRay. Your ex now looks so much better than you remembered. Their words are kinder, the sex is hotter, and of course the fights were fewer, almost non-existent.

Smoke and mirrors my friends, fucking CGI at its worst. You might as well be blue, catlike and running around the goddamn rainforest playing basketball and smoking cigarettes. It's not even that it's good, it's just really, really well marketed.

So you'll trick yourself until you can't even remember what's real and what has been enhanced. You're the one who wanted out, and you had so many good reasons as to why! Can't you remember them now? Not even one? We've gone over them a thousand times!

Look, remember the time he…
He didn't really mean it though.

Well how bout the time he…
Well, he said he was sorry for that.

I know, but you never liked when he use to…
But he's gotten so much better.

I suppose, but he's such a dick to you…
Well, I'm not perfect either.

Do you think it's ever going to change?
Not if we don't try, it's not!

And just like that, you relapse.

Intervention time...

Is breaking up hard to do? No, not really. Is getting out clean? Yep, it's almost impossible. Who hasn't done the on again, off again a hundred times? You'll drive your friends crazy, wasting so much time talking about it, as if their opinion really carries any weight at all. Break ups test our limits; they push us to the edge. You may find yourself driving by someone's house, or by their work, just to hopefully catch them in a lie so that you can finally close the book on them for good.

So there you are, sitting in your car, headlights off as if you're working for the feds doing undercover surveillance. Waiting... staring... smoking... I thought you quit? The radio is off and... wait... shhhhh, don't move... don't fucking move... was that movement by the upstairs window... I repeat upstairs window... hold on... nope... it's just the wind, stand down girls, I repeat STAND DOWN... it's a false alarm.

What the hell has happened to you anyway? You're going to make yourself crazy! You sit there and read all the old saved text messages over and over again like they're suddenly going to somehow change? There's no simple way to ease the pain of it. I know the withdrawal can be overwhelming; you've simply got to detox yourself. With time, you'll become your good old self again, I promise.

Many girls think that finding another guy is the best answer to moving on. I wish I could say that works, but you know it won't, and so do I. By adding another person to your situation, you'll just end up making the whole mess so much bigger. You're hurting right now, I know. I've been there. Trust me, we've all been there.

If you really want to get better, and get clean once and for all, well then you're going to have to beat this one alone. You can try and get help from family and friends, but it's going to come down to you just sweating it out of your system... alone.

How long will this take?

Some people have tried to come up with cute little charts to explain exactly how long. Six months for every year that you spent together is a common one.

For example: If you dated for three years, you'll be moved on and feeling better in about eighteen months. The problem is, that just like being a drug addict, the addiction will always be there. I don't think that we're ever totally cured. For some people, it's much worse than for others. I can tell you that with me, I always feel like I'm one sip away from going on a major ex-girlfriend bender.

I have to stay away completely from a few of my former girlfriends just for fear of having a bad "relapse." (Beth, you're not on that list, get over yourself.) It's not that I want to be with them again or that I can't handle them being with someone else. I think it's the feeling of knowing that if I went back to that, all of the hard work would already be done. See with an ex, they already know all your quirks and problems. With a new person there tends to be so much bullshitting in the beginning that the fakeness can be just exhausting. That's why a lot of people end up going back to an old relationship over and over again.

But you can't.

Why?

One, you don't really want to be back together. And two, if you do, it becomes like using steroids in sports. An asterisk is now placed next to both your names: Becky and Jeff were deeply in love.[*]

   No matter how good things may seem on that second go around, there remains that nasty little reminder that it was far from solid during your first run together. It was far from "meant to be." In other words, your love was not 100% true. That's the nail in the coffin for any relationship. Suddenly realizing that what you two had wasn't in fact... perfect. It wasn't *The Notebook*, it wasn't a love story, and it wasn't... without asterisks.

---

[*] Becky & Jeff in love: From Dec 2009 – Jan 2010, then again from Jun 2010 – Nov 2010.

But Daddy I Love Him!!!

Shouted the little fish girl at her father. No daughter of mine will marry a human! The tricky part about break ups (especially for girls) is that they're disguised as romantic, when, really, they should be your cue to pay the check and say goodnight for the very last time. Really though, who wants a guy that won't fight for you?

Healthy, happy relationships are really wonderful. But the dramatic, intense, dysfunctional ones are way more fun. Even if you say that you don't like the drama (which I've heard from some of the most dramatic women I've ever met), part of you truly does associate it with real love.

I'll never stop loving you…

Here is a list of some couples that you may have heard of before:

Noah & Allie
Bella & Edward
Romeo & Juliet
Johnny & June
Big & Carrie
Queen Victoria & Albert
Aladdin & Jasmine
Jen & Brad
Brangelina
Tristan & Isolde
Dorothy & Jerry
Buttercup & Wesley
Beauty & The Beast
Taylor & Drew
Rose & Jack
Paris & Helen of Troy

Ross & Rachel
Landon & Jamie
Harry & Sally
Rick & Ilsa
Baby & Johnny
Lady & The Tramp (Did he have a name?)

Ok, now, try to pick out the couple- or love story- that's not based on breaking up, fighting or heartbreak.

Kind of scary, huh?

You see it now, don't you? We've decided as a culture that true love involves drama, heartache and strife. From real people to cartoons and now even vampires, all the best love stories have been about everything crumbling to pieces, before love and fate find a way to save the day. The scariest part for me is that young girls are fed this shit from such a young age. If our parents were fed this message as an afternoon snack, we were fed it as three-course meal. How young? Very young. One of the first full sentences that I ever heard from my niece was,

"But Daddy I love him!"

Cute, right? She was pretending to be Ariel, fussing at her daddy about being in love with the human boy, Prince Eric. She was also two years old and had already equated true love with drama. I think that we all secretly crave it a bit. We need it because true love is worth fighting for, right?

Well good luck overcoming that message. Maybe it's just the way things are now. It seems to me that even with the couples from the list, it was always the same old song. Well, if we've learned anything from Chris Brown, it's that he beats women, and nothing lasts for... ev...ev...ever, for... ev...ev...ever, not even true love.

This is why we need to become much better at breaking up with one another. If it's over, then it needs to be over. But we seem to always hold on, like there aren't seven billion people living in the world. Well, there are, and we can't be afraid to meet a few of them now and again.

To repeat a statistic from earlier: To get married only one time in your life, which is something that we'd all like to do, means that you will have to break up with 99.999999% of the people that you date. You have got to under-stand that fact if you're going to be successful in dating. It means that there should be way more books about breaking up, and far fewer about fixing broken relationships. Un-fortunately, the opposite is true.

Do you want to get married? Do you want to stay married? You've got to become less picky in the dating part, and much pickier in choosing. In other words, be less picky about who gets a first date, and way choosier in which people you allow to have a second.

Breaking up is only hard because we let a two-month relationship somehow survive three years. Of course it's not easy to get out of that. How many times have you said, "I wish he would just break up with me. I do love him, just not like that anymore."

What kind of love or friendship includes wasting time with someone? You can agree that you'd want the truth too, right? How long would you want a guy to stay with you, just out of pity? How long would you want him to say, "I love you" and not really mean it? How long should he pretend to be "into you" just to avoid hurting your feelings?

Anyone Will Do...

It's just like Kanye West said before he lost his fucking mind, "Having money's not everything, not having it is."

The same goes for girls when it comes to love. Having love's not everything, not having it is.

One theory that I came up with for this book is that girls would rather have "somebody" than "nobody." It's hard to argue against this concept since most women are often never really 100% single, starting from the time they're six years old. Blame it on Disney, I suppose. The fear starts early and is practically carved right into a little girl's head and heart, branded in her mind.

A girl... being alone? Really not ok!

Little girls are asked by a group of gushing women, "Do you have a boyfriend?" When the child replies in her sweet, innocent voice, "Yes..." The excited ladies follow it up with... "Well, is he cute?"

Try and tell me that you've never been a part of this or have never seen it happen. Don't feel bad, you're only doing it because it was done to you. From first grade on, little girls are aware that getting a boyfriend is on the list of shit to get done yesterday. I remember being little, sitting in school on Valentine's Day. We had to decorate shoeboxes and cut a slit into the top of the box so that we could collect our valentines from our fellow classmates. Imagine, an entire classroom of little children, sitting over their bright pink and red construction paper-covered boxes, with safety scissors, glue sticks and sticky tape... carefully sorting through their cheap, store-bought cards. Disney characters and heart stickers everywhere! Little kids stressing out over what to say, and how to say it. Who do I want to "BE MINE?"

Your Pink Box...

Be mine? How controlling is that? MINE!

By the end of the day, little girls were often devastated and in a mad dash to get back home to have girl talk with Mommy. The little boys though? They didn't have a clue what just happened.

Why in the world does anyone think it's cute to have little girls telling little boys that they "love" them, at four and five years old? Or for them to say that they have boyfriends? I think this shit starts way too young. Girls are on a quest to find a man as early as three. Well, American girls are anyway, and I have to wonder if in the midst of some far off jungle, somewhere under a shaded canopy of thousand foot tall trees, do the little tribe girls pressure the little tribe boys from two rivers over to be their boyfriends at five? God, I hope not!

We force this down our little girls' throats and then we wonder why they don't choose better when their time comes to date for real. From the time they're tiny little girls they believe that they're in a "relationship" or breaking up from one. This goes on until the day they marry.

Somebody, instead of nobody, makes more than just good old sense, it becomes a mantra to live by. It's a feeling as strong as right and wrong. Having somebody is right, and having nobody is wrong.

With this entire heartbreak warfare going on, where are the boys? Where do they fit in? Well, boys didn't care about much else besides sports, trucks, guns and super-heroes. We dreamed big and role-played for sure, but when we role-played, pretending to be, say, army guys, superheroes, or sports stars, guess what the very last thing we pre-tended to do was?

Be married or pretend to have babies; superheroes don't have babies!

I don't think I have to tell you, what girls play is very, very different compared to boys. It's just wild how different it really is. Girls play with their toy kitchens and vacuums, and they're always down to play some "house." Playing house means that someone will be the mommy and someone will be the daddy, even if there are only two girls playing. And there's always a little baby to feed. Having a baby doll is a must-have for little girls. Tell me what little American girl's room isn't stocked full with princess stuff? We don't even have a monarchy in the United States, so without having any kings or queens to idolize, I wonder where they get that from? Little boys aren't running around pretending to be princes or kings, are they?

And no little girl ever pretends to be the single, divorced mom when she's playing house with her friends!

So starting at about two years old, it seems that girls are already searching for "The One," and guys are just looking to score... in baseball, soccer, football or basketball. All this pressure and fear is so ingrained into our little girls' heads, that the thought of being Barbie in a big dream house, all alone with no Ken to lay naked on, is simply unbearable to them. So our little girls go through the rest of their lives making sure they have somebody over nobody, and it's not just a silly thought in their heads, it's a LAW to live by!

By the way, that's why V-day sucks for guys. It has nothing to do with our relationship or the love that we have for you. It's really just about the fact that your pink shoebox didn't have as many "Be Mine" cards in it as the little girl who sat next to you. She instantly became a slut and you got your tiny little heart broken, and now I'm stuck buying candy and necklaces for the rest of my fucking life? No thanks.

Ten

Why I'll Never be Getting Married...

If you are happily married at the moment, that's great. I'm so happy for you. Really. If we ever meet each other, you can tell me all about the day, the dress and shoes. Manolo Blahniks! At a wedding, really? I think I should tell you right now that this chapter is not going to be for you. Just skip it (never quite caught on because a real jump rope was just better). 50% of you can read it when you file for your first divorce and around 60% of that same half can re-read it after your second divorce. For the rest of us though, I will explain in depth why I'll never be getting married.

If you have no interest in this, that's fine, I can't say that I really blame you. Blind eye, deaf ear, it's so much easier that way. But if you do decide to read this chapter, and you get pissed off at me, don't say I never gave you the choice. Let's make one thing clear, this chapter is based upon logic and fact. Not opinion.

Several of the girls I've dated made the mistake of asking me whether or not I believed in marriage, or if I thought I'd ever get married. Then once I'd explain my feelings to them in detail, we'd usually break up. Our friends and family would always ask me, "So what was wrong with that one?"

So I wrote this chapter to answer those questions. But after it was written, I sat on it for a while. I just couldn't make up my mind as to whether or not it should be included in this book. The deciding factor came from the fact that every time someone heard about this book there were always tons of questions, but the two that kept coming up over and over again were:

"What's your book about?"

And

"So do you believe in marriage?"

I felt that by leaving this chapter out of the book, it would only cause me to have twice as many emails to respond to somewhere down the road, and since I figured that I may not feel like doing that then, I'd might as well just put it all out there now.

I'd also like to add that this chapter dives head first into the history of marriage and its ties to organized religion. It's safe to say that you may be offended heavily during some of it, a few of you on many different levels. Although, if you've already made it this far, I think that you'll be just fine. By the way, God told me to write this chapter ☺.

Just Like Ripping Off a Band-Aid...

I was out the other day meeting up with my friends to have a drink and catch up. Catching up always seems to be this big ordeal. Like sitting on the bleachers in the chatty moms' section at a soccer game. Or what I imagine it's like to hang out with the mothers who sign their tiny daughters up for those creepy fucking beauty pageants.

This person said this, that person did that, how lucky, how sad, blah, blah, blah, blah.

"Did you hear about the baby?"
"I can't wait to see their baby."
"What did she do to her hair?"
"He's got a lot of money!"
"I can't believe that he hasn't asked her yet!"
"Oh my God, where's the baby?"

Look, most of the time I do my very best to be polite, I nod and act supportive for my friends because that's the right thing to do, isn't it? I get it, most of the time they're only really asking me so that I can take their side on things. Everyone wants you to agree with whatever it is that they've already decided to be the one right thing. The problem I have though is when they ask me directly, at point blank range, with nowhere safe to hide. "Well what do YOU think about it, D?" I can't help myself. Something happens inside me every time. I answer that question as if the person who just asked it really wanted the honest truth. I do it even though I know better, and I really *do* know better. I swear to you my parents raised me well, but I just can't seem to help myself.

Sure, I have a lot of strong opinions like anybody else does, but I've reached that point in my life where I have no real interest in pushing them onto my friends. Unless of course, they ask me to. Pushing them onto strangers though? Sure, why the hell not? That's this entire book really, and that's fine because it works so much better that way. It's always easier to be honest with a complete stranger than with your friends. That's because when a friend asks you for your advice about something, you have a hard choice to make. Just like ripping off a Band-Aid, there are really only two schools of thought on this:

Rip it off fast, or do it slow and gentle.

You can do your very best to give a clean, constructive answer, but it never really goes as planned. I fall into the truth trap every time, because I'm a rip it off fast kind of guy.

"So Amber and Chris are getting married, what do you think about that?"

Palms sweating... heart-thumping... mouth is going dry... don't do it... don't do it D... shit... here it comes...

"I think he'll cheat on her or she'll let herself go and gain a bunch of weight, most likely both, and after their second kid they'll probably get a divorce."

-Crickets-

"So, wow, I guess that you don't believe in marriage then?"

Damn, they just did it again. Direct question. Must resist... feeling weak...

"Um, not for them, no."

"Well, what about for you?"

"Oh, me? Well, I'm not likely to take a wife."

That wasn't everything that I wanted to say, but it did the job at least. Do I believe in marriage? Sure, kind of. But I'm not really sold on whether or not it's real. All the evidence suggests that it's a big farce, so I guess I can't really say for sure. Just the fact that people can ask the question, "Do you *believe* in marriage?" makes me skeptical. If marriage were a concrete, substantial practice, there would be no reason to use the word *believe* in the question. I'd like to note that I do, however, believe in Bigfoot, aliens and Tupac Shakur (he's still alive, I saw that shit on YouTube).

Will I ever get married?

Uh, no I won't. But that doesn't mean you shouldn't.

"Marwiage, marwiage is what bwings us together today."
-The Princess Bride.

So Then, on to Why I'll Never be Getting Married...

My poor, dear, sweet mother. This is no doubt going to be her least favorite chapter of the book. It's probably noteworthy to mention that my parents are still happily married. They've been happily married now for over 35 years, and they love and care for one another to a level that deserves a standing ovation. More than noteworthy would be my grandparents. They've now been married for over 65 years. That's a long time. It's beyond inspiring to me, and I'm grateful to have seen it first hand. So how all of that relates to this chapter is that there are no broken homes here to blame for all my wacky ideas on marriage, so let's just dismiss that theory now.

I do not believe in marriage. The idea of it is nice. A better way to say it would be that what I *thought* marriage was, sounded nice. The problem was that I was dead wrong.

It turned out that I really had no idea what marriage meant. I thought it was all very simple. A union between a man and a woman. But no, it's much more complex than that. I thought it was also something that you did in a church because God wanted you to. Well, I was wrong again, but before you go burning this book at your church, with *Harry Potter* part nine, please allow me to explain.

The biggest problem is the concept of "marriage," now means (well actually, it always has meant) so many different things in so many different places to so many different cultures. It's difficult to know what it actually is, or how to do it the "right" way. It seems that everyone likes their marriage a little different, almost like coffee, and with so many variations it's almost fitting now to ask, how do you take it? In other words,

"How do you take your marriage these days?"

-Man and woman at a drive-thru-

Intercom Voice: Welcome to The Marriage Lounge, home of happy marriage... How do you take your marriage sir? Will you be trying one of our summer marriage combos today?

Man: Uh no, no thank you...

Intercom: Ok, well go ahead with your order when you're ready, sir.

Man: Yeah, listen, uh, give me a number two, with a six year no-fault clause, and uh... hey, do you guys still have the marital rape exemption here or is that over now?

Intercom: Are you talking about the exemption where you can legally rape your wife because the law says that you own her? No sir, I'm sorry, we actually discontinued that in 1984.

Man: 1984? Really? Ok... Well, let's see, my fiancée is black, does that cost extra?

Intercom: No sir, no extra charge. In fact we're proud to say that since 1967 we were one of the very first Marriage Lounges

in the Northeast to legally honor inter-
racial unions.

Man: Perfect, alright look I also need a...
I'm sorry can you hold on a sec...
honey what? A checking account, and
a car loan... Ok... uh, hey, hello you
still there?

Intercom: Yes, go ahead sir.

Man: Hey my lady's asking me about a
checking account, but my brother had
said y'all don't do checking accounts
in the wife's name? Is that right?

Intercom: No sir, we do, I think he may be confused with the state of Maryland. Here
in Connecticut, a married women has
been able to have her very own checking account without her husband's
written permission since 1974... I'm
sorry, my mistake, 1975.

Man: Perfect. Ok then, we'll add one of
those checking account deals.

Intercom: Ok sir we'll have the total ready for
you at the next window.

-End Scene-

I wish I were joking. Those are just a few of the laws that the
courts were still honoring less than 50 years ago. I always
assumed that because you were married in a church with a

preacher of some sort that it was all a very holy thing. But getting raped legally by your husband, or needing his written permission to open your own checking account? That sounded pretty much like modern day slavery to me. I just couldn't believe that any church would support something like that. I mean all right, maybe sometime way back in the day, but certainly not from anytime that was recent, and as recent as the last fifty years? No way, it was just a bit too crazy to believe.

So I decided I'd look a bit closer and take a fun Google field trip, no permission slips needed here! I'll tell you what I found in just a second, but first let me explain briefly what I thought marriage was really about.

Going to the Chapel, Shit, Stop the Car...

My basic understanding of marriage was that it was a public proclamation, a ceremony held before a congregation, family and God. A truly beautiful concept. And don't forget those meaningful, straight-from-the-heart words, the ones that are supposed to be honored for all of time: The wedding vows. Now that's the real cherry on top.

For better or worse, in sickness and in health, for richer or poorer (that's the best one), 'til death do we part, or until we get bored.

That concept would be perfect for me, if only it were real. Even better would be if it were something taken so seriously that it was punishable by death for breaking! Now there's a concept I could get behind!

Death for breaking your wedding vows?

Yup, I'd say that's more than fair, because look, while I've never actually had any children (thank you Trojan), from what I understand, losing them feels as close to death as it gets, and for a guy, having your children go to live with another man... well that's more of a slow death feeling, like being tortured in one of those fucked up *Saw* movies. Even worse than that though, is getting the boot from your wife, and having to still pay the bills, all while another man raises your children (and fucks her in your first home). Listen you'd might as well die, be resuscitated and then punched in the face a few times, then left to die again.

I decided that maybe my problem was that I just didn't understand the word's meaning. Maybe somehow I'd gotten it all mixed up? So I looked it up.

Marriage[*] – [**mar**-ij] –noun. A social union or legal contract between individuals that creates kinship. An institution in which interpersonal relationships, usually intimate and sexual, are acknowledged in a variety of ways, depending on the culture or subculture in which it's found.

I still didn't get it. I thought it was about having a relationship, but it reads more like a contract for a new car? I also thought that "marriage" was supposed to be an activity, something you can do or have.

"We have a good marriage."

I believed it was something that changes over time, and it could get better, or could get worse. It should be a verb. An action to be performed, ongoing, like say, the act of gardening:

We are gardening… we are marriaging? Is that even a word?

See it doesn't quite work. The closest to that is maybe, "we are marrying," or "we are married." But that seems to indicate a one-time event (like a wedding). It's clearly an ongoing activity though, so the word "married" seems wrong to me somehow. It's a process, not a single event.

The wedding though, now that's a one-day, half-hour event. The marriage, that's a life-long activity. It needs to be explained better. You don't garden once. It wouldn't work. It's *gardening*. The word's actual meaning is very

---

[*] Definition from Wikipedia

important. How else could anyone ever consider doing something that has such huge responsibilities and conesquences (especially in the event of its very possible failure) without first fully understanding what the word itself actually means?

This was all way too confusing for me, so I switched my focus over to love. I liked the idea of it being about love. It felt better, brighter, and a bit more Nicolas Sparks-y to me, so that made more sense. Let's go with love. What you really wanted was to love somebody, and have him or her love you back and then spend the rest of your days growing old together.

So what was wrong with the idea of it being about love? Well, nothing really, except that if it was really just about love, shouldn't everyone be able to do it?

Two men, or two women?

Why should it really matter one way or the other? Since when did love have so many rules and boundaries anyway? I thought the whole mantra was that love could never be wrong? Jesus taught love, and Lennon (who thought he was Jesus) said it was all you really need. It does seem to matter though. It matters to the church, and it matters to the state, and Lord knows there are no queers in either of those places!
I know that you may not want to get into all of this, but it won't take that long, and it's crazy important. I won't drag it out, and I'll make it incredibly simple for you to digest. It's all leading somewhere very exciting, I promise.

Only Fools Rush in...

If an Elvis preacher can do it for you in Vegas, can it really be that big of a deal?

1. The real reason, and only reason, that people are against gay marriage is biblical, period.

2. Marriage in our country is a secular concern, not a religious one, despite what your mother or priest might say.

3. In other words, no married couple's *legal* vows are defined by the word of God. Not in the red words or the black ones.

So what does this all really mean?

It means that all of your handwritten vows, and cute kissing fish that swam around in perfect bowls on the guest tables, and even the DVD combo pack that you had especially made (so that you could watch yourself play princess over and over again) are not binding in any way, shape, or form.

Stay with me here because it's going to get a bit bumpy.

Even all nine of your bridesmaids at the church, and all the rest of the guests who were there, have no impact on your legal wedding (except for the witness' signature). This is because while a church ceremony is sweet (and one of the ten times some of you will ever go to a church), it isn't required for a legal marriage. You're only actually legally married when you both sign the legally binding contract that's required by the state- a binding contract that has become so frail these days, you would never stand for its outrageous looseness if it governed selling your own property or business.

So it's the courts that must "approve" your marriage, not the pastor, church, congregation, or God... because you don't pay God taxes. The whole thing really comes down to money (taxes), property (taxes) and children (again taxes). It was the only reason the courts ever got involved in marriage (as we define it today) in the first place.

When you get married and come together to form a union, money, property and children often follow. These items, like everything else, must be organized for a society to work.

So enter the courts to keep it all "straight" (no pun intended). The government had enough going on without having to support random babies and babies' mommas, and babies' momma's mommas, so in an attempt to keep it all neat and tidy they got involved with the affair of marriage way back in the day, mostly to ensure that people were held accountable if, and when, the love ever died off.

Don't argue with me, you can Google that shit if you feel like it.

That doesn't really explain the church yet, does it? We're getting there.

But first, let's get back to the gays! You know that *Ellen* wasn't always allowed in your living room, and girls didn't always kiss their roommates in hot tubs on TV either. It was the church, not the government, which saw to that. The government as a whole, I mean as an institution, didn't give a flying fuck about the gays, and I'm fairly sure that they still don't, the same way they don't really care what you or I do. You can do almost anything as long as you still pay your taxes.

Have eighteen kids, drill for oil, pan for gold, plant a farm, cut your own face open, abort your baby, even change your sex, but you'd better pay your taxes! Even with marijuana in California now, you may grow it, sell it and smoke it, just pay your fucking taxes!

So then, why no gays allowed? Once upon a time there were a few individuals in the government (who also desperately needed more votes to stay in office) that realized the churches had lots and lots of eligible- and more importantly- obedient voters.

Let the hate games begin!

What does this have to do with you? Nothing yet, remember, this whole chapter is supposed to be about me! No really though, if you can't see what it has to do with you and everyone else, well then you're a moron! So skip ahead, there are at least two more Lady Gaga jokes left to go.

To the rest of you, what have we learned so far? Gays can't marry because if they did, the crooked politicians would lose their Bible thumping votes. In other words, lose their political jobs. Yes, the gays still have to pay their taxes, they can buy houses, go to McDonald's, host TV shows, and raise babies, but they just can't get married everywhere yet because the Bible kind of, sort of says somewhere, that it might be "morally" wrong.

Well "morally" and "legally," at least in this case, are contrasting words. Think about it for a second. No legal human right that you're entitled to as an American citizen is decided upon, affected by, or determined by the church.

"Brothers and sisters can I get an Amen and
a thank you baby Jesus for that fact!"

Their wacky "moral" compass has no say in your rights as a human being.

NONE.

The same church that didn't consider marriage as a "holy" practice for almost ten centuries, and especially didn't view it as the appropriate choice morally, is now deciding who should be allowed to marry and who shouldn't? Despite the fact that the church has no "legal" say or "legal right" to be involved in your marriage they have somehow declared themselves experts on which people's love should count?

Well I have something to say about that… shocker (drink bitch). Brace yourself.

The same church that protects, and continues to employ pedophiles? The church that worries that *Harry Potter* will ruin your dear child's mind and soul, but then allows people to play Chris Brown's music during their "religious" wedding ceremony? They won't allow Tom and Tim to get hitched?

Really?!

It truly amazes me that the same church that has been responsible for more death, deceit and devastation than even our own government, still feels they have the right to hold a moral high ground on any fucking subject. Come on.

Jesus and His + 1

Well let me give you a few brief fun facts about the church and its history of marriage:

Jesus never got married. He was 33 years old and still single, yet my mom's been on my ass about it since I was 25! The Son of God, however, never married.

So simmer down Mom.

Of course, other people back then did sometimes marry. Jewish priests in fact were required to be married. Christians didn't much care for marriage though. Like I said before, for almost ten centuries it was viewed as an immoral, dirty, sure-fire, one-way ticket to hell.

In holy wedded matrimony? Bullshit. The only thing the early Christians even worried about was the end of the world. You see Christianity is an apocalyptic religion. That means that way back in the day their only method of getting new customers was through recruitment. You had to be born Jewish to be Jewish, but if you wanted to become a Christian, just dunk your head in some water and take a vow. Everyone was completely consumed with going on to heaven, and being married wasn't on the official list of immunizations needed to get through those pearly white gates. Who had time to shop for white dresses when they had the rapture to prepare for?

While Judaism was all about marriage, the Christians had other more pressing shit to worry about. End of days shit. So after Jesus, Saint Paul decided he wasn't Jewish anymore, and he wrote this letter to the Corinthians, basically saying don't touch girls, no fooling around, no sex, keep it in your pants buddy...

"It's not good for a man to touch a woman."

The guy was a major cock block by the way.

"Art thou loosed from a wife? Seek not a wife."

It was his opinion that people would be happier if they never married. He believed that marriage was acceptable but still immoral. Does this Saint Paul character sound familiar? No, it can't be... this isn't the same letter that is read at countless weddings, is it? Yep, you nailed it. In the very same letter, a mere six chapters later, Saint Paul goes on to say this:

> Love is patient,
> Love is kind and is not jealous;
> Love does not brag and is not arrogant,
> Does not act unbecomingly;
> It does not seek its own,
> Is not provoked, does not take into account a
> wrong suffered,
> Does not rejoice in unrighteousness, but
> rejoices with the truth;
> Bears all things, believes all things, hopes
> all things, endures all things.
> Love never fails;

He was talking about God though, not the love you feel for your partner. Still happy you had your sister read that at your wedding? Sorry.

He loosened up later finally rationalizing,

> "Let them marry, for it is better to marry
> than to burn with passion."

Yikes! So it seems that the church wasn't going to have my answers. God played a role in it of course, but the churches were making a complete hot mess of the rest. I needed to keep on looking.

Does Your Marriage Have a Late Fee?

If it isn't about love then, and definitely not about religious vows, maybe it was really just about commitment? Ok, I'll bite. What kind of commitment though? There are all different kinds. A real commitment is hard to break. I'll give you some examples: a cell phone contract, a car loan, a military service agreement or a gym membership. All four are harder to break than a marriage contract these days. Our society has made it easier to end a marriage than to quit your local gym. Imagine if you walked into your gym and asked to speak to the manager and said,

> "I think I'm unhappy working out here. It was great in the beginning, I was so in love with this place, but now I've found a new gym, with better equipment and a smoothie bar! So I've decided that I'm going to quit this gym. However, because I'm used to having a gym to go to everyday and I'm also used to all the perks this gym has offered me, well, I'd like you to pay for my new gym membership. I've been a member here for the last six years, so I need you to cover at least that long at the new place, it's only fair!"

Now imagine the gym manager saying,

> "Uh, ok sounds good to me."

No gym in the country would agree to that, and do you want to know why? Because it's fucking crazy talk, that's why! But that's the basic idea behind "no-fault divorce" or "unilateral divorce." You only have to cite general discontent with your marriage to be granted a hearing. In other words, if you don't want to be married anymore, that's fine, you may leave. How the other person involved feels about it has no bearing whatsoever it.

Back in the day, you'd need a real reason to get divorced, and then you'd have to be able to prove that reason beyond a shadow of a doubt in court. Someone was always to blame, and someone was always the victim, which meant that if the other person wanted to, he or she had a fighting chance to save their marriage.

> "She committed to me, I don't want to give up on us!"

> "I don't want to lose my family, please Judge help me!"

> "He said for better or worse, I want to keep trying!"

> "My kids need their mother!"

That makes good sense to me, that's how things should be. A good mother or father says that if you want to quit the cheerleading or soccer team, that's fine, but you'd better have a damn good reason for it. You don't just quit and simply say, "I don't like it anymore." We used to be a culture of people who'd never quit and never give up. We've made it so easy now to quit a marriage that it's almost messier to fire someone from your company than it is to divorce them. So what no-fault divorce really means is that now you can't even save your own marriage because the law says that only one person has to want out. If he or she wants out, it's over, period.

The idea of a long-term "legal" commitment means nothing now, and goes right out the window. The only thing worse would be if there was some kind of incentive to get divorced. Man, that would really suck.

Wait, uh, I forgot about alimony. Shit, I always do that.

Alimony, permanent alimony, no-fault alimony! Do you like porn? Google those terms and see some people really getting fucked. One-sided alimony means that someone is getting paid, and the other person is shelling it out.

So if the wife says,

Wife:	I don't like being married to you.
Husband:	Let's talk about this, please.
Wife:	No thank you dear.
Judge:	Good, then it's settled, you need to pay for her new life, with her new man.
Husband:	But Judge, her new man is my co-worker!
Judge:	Sorry buddy, tough break. That's how it goes. Just be glad you get shared custody.

My stomach hurts.

Look, all I'm saying is that it's not really set up to be successful, especially without having a binding commitment. What is marriage without a commitment? It's nothing. It's like playing house, which you're free to quit as soon as you get bored. If the chance to lose your children, your income, and your mind isn't reason enough to run out right now and start looking for rings, I don't know what is.

Double Down on 10

You've heard it said over and over again that fifty percent of marriages now end up in divorce. It's impossible to find a perfectly accurate percentage, but I'm sure it will be even higher by the time this book comes out. If it's true though, that percentage still doesn't include the number of "other" non-married couples who are also breaking up with each other. I'm not saying that it's completely hopeless out there, but what I'm suggesting is that the chances are very high that you'll find somebody to date or marry who thinks it's okay to quit, okay to give up, okay to cash it all in. That being said, with the risk being so high and likely, it's a really huge gamble.

Is it enough to persuade me?

Look, I don't even like scratch offs, I think that they're complete bullshit! No matter how many winners are up there on the gas station wall, the odds are just too high of losing for me to even play. Even raffles and roulette are too much for me. Casino odds are never 50/50 (like marriage) and yet people still play, so maybe if we give you 1 in 2 odds, you'll go for it…

So let's try out some percentages:

Would you get on an airplane if there were a fifty percent chance it would crash?

Would you visit a country with your children, say somewhere in South America, where the kidnapping rate is at fifty percent?

Would you put all of your savings into a stock if there were a fifty percent chance of losing half?

Would you elect to have a cosmetic surgery where there was a fifty percent chance of you being scarred for life?

Ok, keep all of those same questions, but change it from fifty percent to a forty percent chance of it happening. No? Well how about just a thirty percent chance then?

Checkmate. I win, you owe me a Coke.

But this is marriage! It's different, it's personal. I've known a few gambling addicts who've said the same about craps when they're tossing the dice.

I've heard that most first divorces happen before the age of 25. Well that's good news for me because I'm older than that now, but to lose your children, house, and half of your income all before reaching the age of thirty? That's a lot to get through in one piece. I'm a strong man, and I'm certainly strong willed. I'm both driven and incredibly stubborn, but I'm not crazy, or reckless.

I wear a seat belt in the car, a condom in bed, and have fraud protection on my American Express. For me, the risk is just too high to justify doing it. Even with the one I "love."

Eleven

The Grand Conclusion

Great. So now what? I realize that for some people that last chapter was a bit heavy, and maybe it's not where you thought the book was heading. I mean now that you've made it to the very end, you were probably hoping for some grand conclusion to it all, instead all I talk about is how I don't really believe in being married, that's fucked up, right?

Where's the part of the book that sums it all up? Our clever, yet powerful parting words for you?

Well, here's the thing, it has been over a year and a half since I wrote that last chapter and I'm happy to say that a lot has changed for me since then. I'm now married to an amazing woman, who I have two beautiful children with, and they are the three greatest joys of my life. So I guess that people do change after all...

You know I'm just fucking with you, right?

Look, of course I'm not married. That doesn't mean that you shouldn't be though. For some people it works well, and for others, it just doesn't. It's not quite as simple as finding the "one" and falling in love with them. That's because you will fall in and out of love so many times throughout your life, including with the person you decide to someday marry.

I think the most important thing to remember when dating someone is to be honest with yourself about who you are and what it is that you need from a relationship. The better you understand those two things, the easier dating and eventually marriage will be for you.

So good luck with that,

The End. K, bye!

Why are you still reading?

It's over, go home. That was the end.

What? That wasn't good enough?

All right fine, so you want answers?

I think I'm entitled to them...

You WANT ANSWERS?

I WANT THE TRUTH!

YOU CAN'T HANDLE THE TRUTH!

Fine, I will tell you the secret to all of it. Keep in mind that it may not make perfect sense to you right now, but I assure you, this is what you seek. It is the answer to everything.

Here it is.

> The path you are on is where you are going, and if you stay on it, it is also the path to where you'll end up.

Read it again,

> The path you are on is where you are going, and if you stay on it, it is also the path to where you'll end up.

Let's say that you have two paths to choose from. One of them leads to California, and the other one leads to New York. Well you can't take the path leading to California and expect to somehow end up in New York. When you do arrive in California, it's not fair to then hang out there, hoping the whole time that it will change into New York someday, if only you wait around long enough.

Remember, you were never going to New York. You were going to California. That was the path you were on. That was the path you chose. Get it?

The path you're on is where you're going.

Everyone has an idea of where they'd like to end up-in dating and in life. We wish for these things. The truth is, the path you're on right now will determine where you end up, no matter how much wishing you did along the way.

People make this mistake in relationships all day long: you may want some things, and may need some things, you may assume some things, and you may even have an idea of what you're looking for, maybe you know exactly, without a doubt, what it is you're looking for. But, will the path you're headed on right now, right at *this moment*, lead you to that place?

People get excited. People get overzealous. People get blinded. People get desperate. People change their minds. People lie. It's part of life. The part that doesn't change too much though, is you. You have to learn to see on your own, where the path you're on is truly headed.

Nobody else can do this for you.

It took me a long time to figure all this out. I used to think that it was the girls I was choosing, like maybe I was just picking the bad ones. That was wrong though. That was the wrong way of thinking about it. The girls weren't really my problem. They were, who they were. *I* was actually the problem. I wasn't paying close enough attention to the path I was on. I wasn't looking far enough ahead to where I was bound to end up with those girls. I don't blame them. I blame myself for not realizing where I was going.

I wanted an independent woman... but I was dating a girl who lived at home and got an allowance from her parents. She was never going to be an independent woman. She was looking for another daddy. Somehow, I didn't want to see it.

I wanted a confident woman... but she was always complaining about her body. Always needing compliments. Somehow I didn't hear it.

I wanted a woman who wasn't jealous... but she was always asking to go through my phone and to have my passwords. I ignored it.

I wanted a woman who was ready to settle down with me... but she was a bartender who liked to be out all night. I believed somehow it would change.

I wanted a woman who was honest... but she had cheated on her boyfriend to be with me. I thought I was different.

I wanted a woman who was kind... but when we'd be on the phone she would snap at her own mother. I tuned it out.

I wanted a woman who had her own life... but she made me the only thing that mattered in hers from our second date on.

I wanted a woman who wouldn't lie to me... yet I stayed with her long after I caught her in that first one.

I wanted a woman with strong morals... but I didn't say no to her when she got naked on that first night... or second.

I was the reason. *I* was the one who picked those paths.

Instead of seeing what was clear as day to everyone around me, I was the guy saying:

We're Just Not There Yet

Well the truth was, we would *never* be there. Not the way we were going anyway, and it was so simple as to why.

Because that wasn't the path we were on from our very first step.

The End... for real this time.

P.S. Yes, you look pretty today, and I mean it this time.